C000052416

*Rona Orme is the Children's Missi[...]
lived in a small Devon village for [...]
in 2007. Passionate about working with children and families, [...]
responsible for establishing a new congregation for families with children
under the age of eight in her Devon village, which continues to thrive. She is
the author of* Rural Children, Rural Church *(Church House Publishing,
2007) which explores mission opportunities in the countryside, and*
Creative Mission *(Barnabas for Children, 2011). She is now involved
with leading WoW (Worship on Wednesdays) for children and adults
together in a primary school. Rona is a Reader in the Church of England.*

Barnabas
for
Children

Barnabas for Children® is a registered word mark and the logo is a registered device mark of The Bible Reading Fellowship.

Text copyright © Rona Orme 2013
The author asserts the moral right
to be identified as the author of this work

Published by
The Bible Reading Fellowship
15 The Chambers, Vineyard
Abingdon, OX14 3FE
United Kingdom
Tel: +44 (0)1865 319700
Email: enquiries@brf.org.uk
Website: www.brf.org.uk
BRF is a Registered Charity

ISBN 978 0 85746 148 3
First published 2013
10 9 8 7 6 5 4 3 2 1 0
All rights reserved

Acknowledgments
Unless otherwise stated, scripture quotations taken from the Contemporary English Version of the Bible, published by HarperCollins Publishers, are copyright © 1991, 1992, 1995 American Bible Society.

Scripture quotations taken from The Holy Bible, New International Version (Anglicised edition) copyright © 1973, 1978, 1984, 2011 by Biblica (formerly International Bible Society). Used by permission of Hodder & Stoughton Publishers, an Hachette UK company. All rights reserved. 'NIV' is a registered trade mark of Biblica (formerly International Bible Society). UK trademark number 1448790.

A catalogue record for this book is available from the British Library

The paper used in the production of this publication was supplied by mills that source their raw materials from sustainable managed forests. Soy-based inks were used in its printing and the laminate film is biodegradable.

Printed in Singapore by Craft Print International Ltd

More
Creative
Mission

Over 40 further ideas to help church and community
celebrate special days and events throughout the year

Rona Orme

Acknowledgments

I have had a lot of fun preparing this book; trying out some of the ideas, listening to the experiences of other people who have put on events or tried to do things in a different way, and talking through possibilities with friends and colleagues. I would particularly like to thank Miles Baker, Chris Burnett, Sue Doggett, Sue Fulford, Jenny Parkin, Gillian Spokes, Margaret Withers, the people of the Diocese of Peterborough and everyone who has been involved with Polzeath Family Mission over so many years.

God has blessed me richly through all of these people and I thank him for that.

To God be the glory, great things he has done!

*

Contents

Mission ideas for Spring

Mission ideas for Summer

Mission ideas for any time

Appendices

✳

Foreword

Whether we have been planning missional activities and services for years or it is a newer calling, there are occasions for all of us when the ideas cupboard looks empty; our desire to reach out with the love of the Lord Jesus remains ever strong, but we can't get traction on the specifics. Or maybe after trying something a few times, we feel it isn't connecting and need new ideas with which to experiment.

In *More Creative Mission*, Rona does a great service to God's Church, offering us dozens of imaginative, fun and creative ideas for a host of occasions and contexts. For city, town and village, for churches overflowing with people and those with a handful, there is an abundance of possibilities.

To see this book only as one of practical ideas would be to miss much. Embedded within is a theology that sees mission not as something done to children but as done with and by all ages together. May I suggest not just thumbing to a particular idea but drinking from the wisdom in the 'Frequently Asked Questions' section?

In offering ideas for Christian festivals and other times of significance in the world around us, Rona reminds us of the call to go to others in mission and not expect them to come to us. This is an easy sentiment to espouse, but in providing suggestions for starting where people can connect with the church, Rona shows us what theory can look like in practice.

Undergirding the book is a theology of mission rooted in a sense of God's lavish abundance. At a time when it is easy to feel the best outcome for the church is slightly slower decline, we read a reminder of the One who promises to turn even the barren waters of the dead sea not only fresh but teeming with life (Ezekiel 47). May this book help us and others to know more of this abundant life in Christ.

Revd Barry Hill, Mission Enabler for the Diocese of Leicester

✳

Introduction

What is mission?

Go to the people of all nations and make them my disciples. Baptise them in the name of the Father, the Son, and the Holy Spirit, and teach them to do everything I have told you. I will be with you always, even until the end of the world. (Matthew 28:19–20)

As disciples of Jesus we are invited to join in the mission, the 'sending out', of God. We are the hands, the feet, the smiles and the compassion through which the Holy Spirit can operate. We are of every chronological age because all disciples, however young, are called to join in the work of mission. *More Creative Mission* provides a wide range of suggestions to help churches involve children and families in mission.

One well-tried route to introduce people to the love of God is to invite them to fun social events. There they will have the chance to get to know people for whom the Christian faith is a key part of their lives. Many families may not have close Christian friends, so social gatherings can help them to see faith being lived—a testimony without words. Once good relationships have been built, there comes the opportunity to share the stories of the Bible. It may take many points of contact for someone to move from a position of 'not knowing' to 'knowing about' to 'knowing' Jesus as their Saviour. Each church, every Christian working in mission, every person who knows Jesus can help individuals along that path of discovery. Once people come to faith, it is also the church's role to help them mature in discipleship and take their part in the mission of God. These stages apply to children as much as to adults. Children need to hear the good news before they can respond. They can *be* the good news if they are helped to grow in discipleship and to understand the importance of being involved in sharing the good news of Jesus.

Children can be particularly enthusiastic about mission. They love raising money for good causes and they are often first to point out injustice. They are quick to bring their friends to activities that they themselves enjoy. They are good at persuading parents and carers to get involved. Children who are growing in their faith will often be looking to share that buzz with others. We can provide the opportunities for them to do so. Involving children in the planning and running of events will help them to mature both socially and spiritually. Children thrive when they are allowed to play a full part.

Of course, we should not always expect people to come to us. You will find plenty of suggestions in this book for joining in activities organised by other community groups. We can take the light, salt and yeast of Christ with us into the wider world.

Jesus tells us, 'Every student of the Scriptures who becomes a disciple in the kingdom of heaven is like someone who brings out new and old treasures from the storeroom' (Matthew 13:52).

Everyone who works with children and families needs plenty of ideas to keep their work fresh. *More Creative Mission* is a collection of new and refreshed ideas; some follow the liturgical and seasonal calendar, while others can be tried at any time. The index will help you find ideas for specific occasions, purposes or groups of people as well as suggestions linked to particular Bible verses. While most of the ideas have been tried and tested, do not hesitate to adapt the suggestions for your own purposes or circumstances. Allow the Holy Spirit to excite you as you read!

God blesses those people who refuse evil advice and won't follow sinners or join in sneering at God. Instead, the Law of the Lord makes them happy, and they think about it day and night. They are like trees growing beside a stream, trees that produce fruit in season and always have leaves. (Psalm 1:1–3)

I pray that you will produce fruit in season and know the joy of drawing strength from the living water of Christ.

*

Frequently asked questions

How do we decide which idea to use?

Excitement

As you read through the book, some ideas will excite you more than others. These are the ideas to look at more closely. We all put more effort into doing things that we are excited about. Running events because we think we 'should' will always feel like drudgery.

Skills

The skills and interests of the church family should dictate the ideas that you develop. Churches that are particularly artistic will enjoy 'The Big Draw', 'Preschool project' or 'Bible Sunday' ideas (pp. 43, 180 and 46). Other congregations may prefer bigger, more outward-looking events such as 'Advent windows' or 'Good Shepherd Sunday' (pp. 23 and 29). If a church member is passionate about helping other people to cook, then start with the 'Slow food' activity (p. 147) or 'The Big Lunch' (p. 145). Sometimes it works well to invite someone from outside the church family who has the appropriate skill or enthusiasm to get an event off the ground. In this instance, it is important that they understand that they are being line-managed by a named person with authority within the church.

Calendar

Many of the ideas in this book will take a number of weeks, if not months, to plan and organise. It is important that the planning stage is not skimped. This means that it is a good idea to select an idea for a time some way ahead. Please do not be tempted to stage something for Christmas if it is already November when you pick up this book. My prayer is that you take time to succeed.

Are there any legal requirements to consider?

Safeguarding

It is the responsibility of each church, group leader and individual leader to ensure the safety of children who are left in their care. Think of this as 'granny standard' care: look after the children as if they were your own grandchildren. Legislation requires you to undertake risk assessments for ensuring the health and safety of children and young people, to use consent forms (with contact details and information about medical requirements), and to make sure that no adult is left alone with a child. Ensure that all activities involving children can be easily observed from outside the room. While these procedures may sometimes seem burdensome, they provide an opportunity for us to serve the children entrusted to our care to the highest standard.

www.isa.homeoffice.gov.uk

www.churchofengland.org/media/37378/protectingallgodschildren. pdf (provides helpful advice on legal requirements and good practice)

www.peterborough-diocese.org.uk/safeguarding/safeguarding (to find a code of practice to download for everyone who works with children)

Photography

Parents or carers must give permission before any photograph or video is taken of a child. If children are to be left without their parents, it is good practice to include a question about permission to take photographs (and so on) on any consent form. Use coloured sticky labels to indicate discreetly children who should not be photographed. At events where consent forms will not be used, such as large scale drop-in events where children remain the responsibility of the adult who brought them, it is a good idea to display a notice saying that photographs and video may be used for future publicity purposes. Explain that adults can obtain a coloured sticky label for each child so that photographers know to avoid getting them in frame. Generally, adults are expected to speak up for themselves if they do not wish to be included.

Use of CDs and DVDs

The law permits the use of commercially recorded music within the context of worship without a licence. If CDs or similar are played at other events, it is the responsibility of the organisers to check that the meeting space has an appropriate licence. Full details and advice are available from PRS for Music.

See 'Movie sing-along' (p. 177) for information about the permissions needed to show a full-length movie. However, it is possible to show short clips, lasting up to four minutes, from movies (often those which have been issued as trailers) by using the Wingclips website. Many of these can be accessed for free.

www.prsformusic.com
www.wingclips.com

Data protection

Data covered by the Data Protection Act 1998 includes personal records (such as email addresses, telephone numbers, consent forms and photographs) and entries in accident and incident books. This information must be kept up to date and secure, and used only for the purposes for which permission has been given. It is worth noting that records relating to children's activities, such as attendance registers, should be kept for 50 years after the year to which they relate. Each church denomination should be able to provide more detailed advice in this area.

www.ico.gov.uk

How do we encourage people to take part?

Publicity

Good quality publicity material will attract attention. If you have arranged for a school to send home a leaflet via pupils' book bags, make sure that the leaflet will still look attractive when parents find it. One way to do this is to use postcards that are much less likely to look chewed up. High-quality postcards and business cards can be obtained online for a very reasonable charge from Vistaprint. The website offers a range of templates and the opportunity to edit text boxes to produce professional-style publicity. Similar material, although with less choice and flexibility, can be ordered from Christian Publicity and Outreach. If a good relationship has been built up with a school, ask if the event can be included in the school's own newsletter as this will indicate to parents and carers that the school endorses it to some extent.

www.cpo-online.org.uk
www.vistaprint.com

Posters

People rarely come to an event because they have seen a poster, but it may reinforce an invitation they have already received or confirm the arrangements. Ensure that the image on a poster matches the image on invitations. Make the wording big and bold. If in doubt, cut down the amount of information that appears but give a mobile phone number, website or social media source to consult for more details.

Promotion

Find a way to bring a taste of an event to your target audience. One way to do this is to hand out something along with the invitation. For example, distribute a pine cone or conker with the invitation to the 'National Tree Week' event (p. 68) or a tea light as part of the invitation to mark Remembrance and St Martin's Day (p. 56), so people can bring along the candle to be lit if they wish. Sachets of Fairtrade hot chocolate would be a fun giveaway as part of an invitation to a *Sound of Music* movie sing-along (p. 177) and a pencil or crayon could accompany publicity about 'The Big Draw' (p. 43).

Personal invitation

I enjoy watching films but I rarely go to the cinema. When I do go to the movies it is either because someone tells me that a new film is particularly good or because someone invites me. People will come along to church events if the person inviting them makes it sound attractive and something that they themselves are looking forward to. Make sure that the people who will be doing the inviting are excited about the event and are well-informed about what it will involve. (For example, I like to know how long a film will last and whether my companion wants to go for a pizza afterwards.)

Recent research (see www.nurseryworld.co.uk) has indicated that young parents are more likely to take their baby or toddler to an event if it has been recommended by a friend or relative rather than just seeing some publicity. The same research showed that the main reason for young parents not to return was if they felt that existing members were 'cliquey'.

This research is a reminder for all those hoping to welcome new people that they must work to ensure that people really do feel relaxed and valued. Arrange to have a couple of people whose role is to look out for first-timers and visitors instead of focusing on the needs of the existing group. The only reason that I returned to a toddler group many years ago was because Wendy was on duty to welcome visitors and to keep them company through the first session. I certainly looked out for Wendy the following week as I felt there would be at least one person I knew.

Plan

It is good practice to hand people an invitation to the next event as they leave the current one. This means that it is essential to have at least outline arrangements already decided, such as type of event, date and time, even if the next occasion is some way ahead. Otherwise, if it is ready, hand out the polished invitation with warm encouragement to come back. Point people towards a social media site if you use one to publicise events.

Social media

It is straightforward to set up a Facebook page dedicated to church events, or to highlight one event in particular. Then point people in its direction with a suggestion that they search for 'title of event' on Facebook. In the same way, invite a keen Tweeter to set up a Twitter feed for an event. Do not forget to register events on the WhereCanWeGo website so that people may come across your occasion when they are looking for something to do on a particular date or in a specific locality.

www.wherecanwego.com

Who should we involve... in the church, in the community?

Everyone! One of the best ways of encouraging people to get to know us (and thence to get to know Jesus), is to ask them to help. Many people are flattered to offer their expertise to help an event to happen. There are many instances of people who have been asked to contribute their musical skills by playing in a group, and who have gone on to faith because they have found themselves regularly in church and had an opportunity to hear the gospel. Sometimes standing back from a task that we could easily do ourselves allows someone else to find either a new ministry or even a way into church.

Why are most of the ideas for children and adults together?

I firmly believe that it takes a whole church to raise a Christian (to paraphrase the African proverb). While children need time to be with their own age group (although this is not possible in small churches), they also need to observe the Christian faith in action of older people and to enjoy warm relationships with them.

Another argument for welcoming children and adults together is that when many parents have to use extended childcare during the working week, they often prefer to spend time in the company of their children at the weekend or at social occasions. A third reason is that often parents are none too familiar with Christian beliefs and the account of Jesus' life and ministry. It is less daunting to accompany children than to have to admit to their own low level of knowledge or understanding. They can learn, or refresh the basics, without showing their ignorance.

Some of the ideas are just fun; how are we sharing our faith?

Faith is generally 'caught' rather than 'taught'. This means that most people see the difference that having faith in Jesus makes in other people's lives—and then want what they observe for themselves. Fewer people come to faith solely through reasoned argument or even through hearing the gospel expounded. This means that it is important for Christians to be building relationships and extending their friendship circles as widely as possible. It is less difficult to invite friends and acquaintances from the school gate to a 'Tree Week' event (p. 68) that is based around fun than to a church service. As relationships grow, people can see the testimonies of Christian lives being lived. Then, as they begin to ask questions, it becomes easier to invite them to an event where they will hear the gospel explicitly preached.

We only have a couple of children in our congregation; which ideas are best for us to use?

Many adults will enjoy some of the activities that involve a more visual and kinaesthetic approach, particularly if they understand they are helping to share their faith with children and young families.

For example, lots of people will enjoy the artistic challenge of the shoebox display for Bible Sunday (p. 46) or the spoken responses in the reading for All Saints' Day (p. 51). If the idea suggests a pass-the-parcel or team game activity, there is no reason why adults should not take part. Make it clear that all age really does mean all ages learning and worshipping together, not children doing (or worse, being thought to perform or entertain) and adults watching and even applauding. At the same time, remember that children enjoy the opportunity to reflect in silence if the activity is explained well. 'The Big Draw' (p. 43) is particularly suitable for all ages to work at their own level.

What can we do if we have no children in our church family?

First of all, look out for the children who are not part of your church family. There are very, very few areas that do not have resident children. Research where local children go to school, and then plan an activity that links with that. For example, one church in Northamptonshire knew that all the children were taken by bus to another village for schooling. They planned a club that started as those children arrived back on the bus in the afternoon. They arranged to escort the children to the hall, provided snacks and drinks, and then moved on to a 45-minute club session. It is very popular, not least because parents do not have to get to the bus stop, take their children to the club and then return to collect them. Another way is to plan activities for youngsters who regularly visit grandparents.

A further idea is to campaign and fund-raise for children who live in poverty (both in the UK and abroad), who live with disability or who work as young carers. 1 Corinthians 3:6 reminds us that Paul sowed seeds, Apollos watered them and God helped them to sprout and grow. We can use our talents for fund-raising and hospitality to support work among children in need even if we do not know them by name.

Seasonal activities

✱

Bookmark competition

Date: from the second week of September

Web links

www.lords-prayer.co.uk
www.lords-prayer-words.com

Introduction

This is a simple idea that provides an opportunity to make contact with schools, nurseries, preschools, uniformed groups, businesses and residential homes by inviting people to design a bookmark to illustrate the Lord's Prayer.

Key Bible verse

You should pray like this: Our Father in heaven, help us to honour your name.
MATTHEW 6:9

Bible links

- Psalm 78:4 (we will tell the next generation)
- Matthew 6:9–13 (Jesus teaches the disciples how to pray)
- Hebrews 5:7 (God listened to Jesus' prayers)

Key focus: Building community relationships; sharing the Christian story

Key group: Children; church family; families; local community; schools; uniformed groups

Activity ideas

Arrange a competition for people to design a bookmark to illustrate the Lord's Prayer. Explain that the Lord's Prayer has been the main prayer of the Christian Church for 2000 years and that you know it is still of great relevance today.

In your promotional material (which could be paper fliers, posters, Facebook page, website and so on), give the text of the prayer and some explanation about where it can be found in the Bible. Local church custom will decide whether that should be in the contemporary or traditional form. Ask for entries to be on paper or card 210 x 124mm (A5, cut in half lengthwise), although you may wish to offer a picture class on A4 paper for children under the age of six. It may also help some people if you provide a template that just needs to be coloured in. Explain that there are a number of classes for entries, such as:

- Best design without words (this is a challenge to capture the essence of the prayer in colour, symbol or pictures)
- Best picture (children under the age of six, see above)
- Best design with the opening phrase 'Our Father in heaven'
- Best design for the whole prayer
- Best decoration of a provided design

You may also wish to divide each class into age categories such as under 7s, 8–11s, 12–17s, adult. Tell entrants to put their name, age (if necessary) and telephone number on the back of their entry. Include the closing date, all the entry categories, details of the exhibition of all the entries, and when the prizes are to be presented.

Give a closing date and arrange, if helpful, to collect entries from schools and so on four weeks ahead of the closing date. It is a good idea to arrange to visit each institution, group or business to explain the concept and to share excitement. Organise an exhibition of all the entries. It may be possible to borrow display boards from a school or local business. Group these according to class (and age group if being used) so that similar items are together and can be compared. Invite someone from outside the immediate area to judge the entries. Provide paper rosettes or similar to indicate the winners in each category.

You may wish to organise a brief celebration at which the prize winners are given small prizes (possibly a small book that features the Lord's Prayer in some way and is appropriate to the age group). It would be fun to sing the Caribbean version of the Lord's Prayer together (*Come and Praise* 51). Invite the local media to the prize giving.

After the event it might be possible to laminate each entry and return it to its designer.

— Prayer —

Lord, teach us to pray, just as John taught his followers to pray.
(Luke 11:1)

Developing the theme

Invite older children and teenagers to illustrate the Lord's Prayer with digital photographs taken around the locality.

*

Advent windows

Date: from Advent Sunday through to Christmas Eve

Web links

http://beyondchurch.blogspot.com/2008/11/advent-beach-hut-calendar.html
www.silentlights.co.uk
www.embracethemiddleeast.org

Introduction

The life-size Advent calendar created in beach huts along the seafront at Brighton was launched in 2008 by a non-traditional church called Beyond. The idea was for the doors of one beach hut in turn to be opened each evening at 6.30pm. Each hut was decorated to encourage reflection on the nativity and each evening highlighted a different Christmas carol that was sung by everyone who gathered.

I live in Northampton, which is far from the sea, and I wondered how this idea could be transported inland. Advent calendars feature windows, so it became obvious that real windows could be used to create the displays. The windows need to be easily viewed from the road and, ideally, somewhere with enough space on the pavement or in the lane for a group of people to gather safely. This idea would work particularly well on a housing estate where the houses are close together. In a village people may be more willing to walk further around at night and it may be acceptable for visitors to enter the front garden to view the display.

Key Bible verse

Sing a new song to the Lord! Everyone on this earth, sing praises to the Lord.

PSALM 96:1

Bible links

* Matthew 1:18–24 (the birth of Jesus)
* Matthew 2:1–12 (the wise men)
* Luke 1:26–38 (an angel tells Mary about the birth of Jesus)
* Luke 1:46–55 (Mary's song)
* Luke 2:1–21 (Jesus' birth and the shepherds)

Key focus: Sharing the Christian story; providing sacred space for reflection; building community relationships

Key group: Church family; schools; local community; families

Activity ideas

Create a numbered list of the venues that will be featured so these can be publicised. Include details of the carols to be sung in your publicity material as this may encourage people to attend to sing their favourite.

Hold a meeting for everyone who is taking part by providing a venue and display so that ideas can be shared and, if necessary, coordinated. Allocate dates, carols and the numbers to be displayed at each venue. If possible, encourage people to choose their favourite carol as they will enjoy illustrating that better. Carols might include:

A great and mighty wonder
Angels from the realms of glory
Away in a manger

Ding dong merrily on high
God rest you merry, gentlemen
Good King Wenceslas
Hark! the herald angels sing
In the bleak midwinter
Infant holy
It came upon a midnight clear
Joy to the world
Little donkey
Long time ago in Bethlehem
Lo, he comes with clouds descending
Mary's boy child
O come, all ye faithful
O come, O come, Emmanuel
O little town of Bethlehem
Of the Father's love begotten
On Christmas night all Christians sing
Once in royal David's city
See amid the winter's snow
See him lying on a bed of straw
Silent night
Tell out, my soul
The angel Gabriel from heaven came
The first Nowell
The holly and the ivy
The Virgin Mary had a baby boy
Unto us a boy is born
We three kings
What child is this?
While shepherds watched their flocks

These carols are given in alphabetical order but they can be allocated to days according to preference. There is no obvious order that can be used to narrate the nativity story.

Explain that each venue needs to create a well-lit display to illustrate the first verse of the carol. The window used can be on the ground or first floor (so flat-dwellers are not excluded). The display needs to be as close to the window as possible, perhaps with closed curtains or a screen behind it to eliminate the visual distraction of the room behind (although this could form an important element of the exhibit). Possible media might include dark paper silhouettes stuck to the window glass; shop mannequins dressed for their role; large puppets; large paintings on board or thick paper. At least one display could consist of commercially available material from Silent Lights (www.silentlights.co.uk). Some people may wish to be part of a living tableau for the 15 minutes of the gathering. However, this means that the exhibit cannot be left on display for the rest of the evening for passers-by to enjoy.

It is important to have a dress rehearsal for each window at least a day before it is unveiled to the public. This will ensure that sight lines can be checked and any problems solved. Ensure that the venue number, as listed on the publicity, is clearly displayed at the venue so that it is easy to see.

Choose a standard time for each window to be unveiled such as 6pm or 6.30pm. To encourage the building of community relationships, advertise that mince pies and Christmas biscuits or other refreshments will be offered at each venue. The refreshments can vary between venues and church families can assist each other in providing refreshments and the exhibit. It is a good idea to have one person responsible for the singing of the carol. This person needs to be positioned outside with the visitors. It may be possible for a trumpeter or other musician who can play in the open air to accompany the carol. A brass quartet would be excellent.

Because of the 'pop-up' nature of this idea, it is important that only one carol is sung each evening (apart from Christmas Eve when different rules may apply). The carol could be sung twice: once at the moment of unveiling or illumination, and once after refreshments have been shared. Provide copies of the words of the carol to be sung. Words of 26 carols can be found on the Bethlehem Carol Sheet produced by Embrace the Middle East (formerly Bible*Lands*). At the end remind everyone of the next venue and announce the carol to be sung there.

Example 1

Joy to the world! The Lord is come;
Let earth receive her King;
Let every heart prepare him room,
And heaven and nature sing,
And heaven and nature sing,
And heaven, and heaven, and nature sing.
ISAAC WATTS (1674–1748)

Display a large inflatable globe, or a printed picture of one, with either a picture or a model of Christ the King attached to it. Around this, arrange as many heart shapes as possible with an image of baby Jesus in a manger in the centre of each. At the base of the display use pot plants to represent nature and add pictures of musical notes to represent nature singing. Above the exhibit display sun, moon, stars and a rainbow and again add musical notes. Cut out the letters J-O-Y and stick these to the window. When the carol is sung, it would be fun to blow bubbles to represent joy coming into the world.

Example 2

Of the Father's love begotten,
ere the worlds began to be,
He is Alpha and Omega,
he the source, the ending, he,
of the things that are, and have been,
and that future years shall see,
evermore and evermore.
AURELIUS CLEMENS PRUDENTIUS (348–C. 413) TRANSLATED BY J.M. NEALE (1818–66)

Arrange a length of fabric to flow from the top left down to the bottom right of the space (looking at the space from the outside). Display a large A (or an alpha symbol or the word 'Alpha') at the top of the 'waterfall' of fabric. Next along the fabric, place a large picture or a model of a heart. The third symbol along the fabric should be a globe, and this will be in the centre of the exhibit. The fourth item should be a large calendar or poster showing the next few years (2014, 2015, 2016). The final symbol, to be placed at the bottom right of the fabric, is a large 'O' (or an omega symbol or the word 'Omega').

— Prayer —

Creator of the world, as so many people prepare to celebrate Christmas, help us to share the light your son brought into the world with our neighbours, friends and family. May we share the joy of Jesus' birth through our carols of praise, our windows of reflection and our gifts of food. Let us join with the angels of heaven who sing, 'Glory to God in the highest.' Amen

Developing the theme

If finding up to 28 venues seems too challenging, start in the first year by finding just four. These can then be unveiled on each Sunday in Advent. If a few more can be found, reveal the extra places on a Friday evening or another midweek night that is appropriate locally. It may well be that after the first year more people will come forward to take part in the event.

Another way to do this would be to have five or six venues on display the same evening and use them as the focus for carol singing around the community.

Finally, this idea could also be used to fund-raise for charity with a collection being gathered at each window display.

*

— An activity for spring —

Good Shepherd Sunday

Date: 4th Sunday of Easter

Web links

www.barnabasinchurches.org.uk
www.embracethemiddleeast.org
www.farmcrisisnetwork.org.uk

Introduction

In the United States, the fourth Sunday of Easter is often known as 'Good Shepherd Sunday' as the lectionary readings for that day always focus on Psalm 23 (You, Lord, are my shepherd) and John 10:7–18 (the good shepherd). While those of us who live in towns may not see many sheep, they are still a popular image. This idea encourages people to be creative in response to Jesus' words. The aim is to share the Gospel passage John 10:1–18, plus other Bible references if appropriate, and invite people to make either their own scene to illustrate one of the Bible references or a sheep to add to a bigger display relating to the good shepherd. Avoid choosing Bible references to sheep being used as sacrifices to God as the imagery has bad connotations for people without a wider understanding of the Bible.

Key Bible verse

I am the good shepherd. I know my sheep, and they know me.
JOHN 10:14

Bible links

- Psalm 23 (you, Lord, are my shepherd)
- Psalm 37:3 (trust in the Lord and enjoy safe pasture—NIV)
- Psalm 65:13 (meadows are filled with sheep... and echo with joyful songs)
- Psalm 78:52 (then God... guided them in the desert like a flock of sheep)
- Psalm 95:7 (we are the sheep God takes care of)
- Psalm 100:3 (we are his people, the sheep in his pasture)
- Isaiah 11:6 (wolves will rest with lambs)
- Isaiah 53:7 (as quiet as a sheep having its wool cut off)
- Ezekiel 34:5–6 (my sheep were scattered across the earth)
- Matthew 7:15 (false prophets... dress up like sheep)
- Matthew 10:16 (I am sending you like lambs into a pack of wolves)
- Matthew 12:11 (If you had a sheep that fell into a ditch on the Sabbath, wouldn't you lift it out?)
- Matthew 25:33 (he will place the sheep on his right and the goats on his left)
- Luke 2:8–20 (shepherds hear about the birth of a Saviour)
- Luke 15:4–7 (the parable of the lost sheep)
- John 10:3 (the sheep know their shepherd's voice)
- John 10:7 (Jesus is the gate for the sheep)
- John 10:1–18 (Jesus is the good shepherd)
- John 21:15–19 (Jesus tells Peter to look after his sheep)
- Acts 20:28 (be like shepherds to God's church)
- 1 Peter 2:25 (you had wandered away like sheep)

Key focus: Building community relationships; sharing the Christian story

Key group: Church family; schools; local community; families

Activity ideas

Produce a poster to advertise your event (see template on page 36). In addition, print copies of the sheet on pages 34–35 to hand out to people who will be coming to the service. The sheets can be made available in church for the weeks leading up to the Good Shepherd Sunday service, and taken to local schools, libraries, community venues and retail outlets along with copies of the poster. The poster and the instruction sheet can be downloaded from the website www.barnabasinchurches.org.uk/extra-resources/.

Start publicising the event at least six weeks in advance so that everyone has plenty of time to create their entry. Plan to have the completed exhibition open for viewing during the week following the service so that schools or preschool nurseries can visit if they wish. Do not charge for entry, although you may wish to sell refreshments at a modest price. Aim to collect donations for an appropriate charity such as Embrace the Middle East or Farm Crisis Network.

Someone of a particularly creative nature may be able to construct a large-scale model of Jesus as the good shepherd to display at the centre of the exhibition. Individual sheep that people make could then become part of the flock gathering around the good shepherd. It would also be fun to create the effect of a sheepfold or gate as people enter the display area. Churches with digital display could project pictures of pasture as a backdrop.

In larger buildings, it may be possible to mount a large area of green paper on to a wall. Then invite people to draw themselves as a sheep, adding their name on to this 'field'. Use the words from John 10:3, where Jesus talks about the shepherd calling his sheep by name, as a caption. Again artistic people may be able to develop the simple green paper into a pasture scene.

Rural parishes could gather wisps of wool caught in hedges or on fences to be made into model sheep to add to the display or to be taken home. Glue round half an empty Smarties® tube or similar and cover it with the wool. Otherwise use wisps of white cotton wool. Cut a black chenille stick (available from craft suppliers, see Appendix on page 195) in half. Wrap each half around the tube and twist underneath to form legs at each end. Add self-adhesive eyes to make a face.

If someone can bring a live lamb to church, that will be a very big draw.

Make sheep-shaped biscuits to offer as part of the refreshments. It might be possible to invite children to decorate theirs with tubes of ready-made icing (or simple water icing) before they eat them.

In the service, make sure to include plenty of sheep references (see Bible links on page 30). Teach the following verse as a memory verse, elongating the 'ee' of the word sheep so that it sounds like a sheep bleating.

He is our God, we are his people, we are the sheep of his pasture (Psalm 95:7, my translation).

Suggested hymns

- Father, hear the prayer we offer
- Loving Shepherd of thy sheep
- One more step along the world I go
- Shout for joy and sing (*The Source* 450)
- The King of love my shepherd is
- The Lord's my shepherd
- The Lord's my shepherd (I will trust in him alone)

To encourage a preschool or nursery to take part in the event (and the children will be enthusiastic makers of craft) offer to visit to read the parable of the good shepherd to the children from a children's Bible, such as *The Barnabas Children's Bible* (Barnabas for Children, 2012).

— Prayer —

Sovereign God, Shepherd and Saviour
Help us to learn to hear your voice.
Each person is precious in your sight and you offer us the gift of
Eternal life with you.
Please, hear our prayer.

Developing the theme

Another way to explore this theme is to invite people to knit, craft or draw a sheep to display in the window of their home or shop. Have a 'hunt-the-sheep' trail for people to track down all the sheep in the area. Finally, invite everyone to bring the sheep they have made to church for Good Shepherd Sunday.

Good Shepherd Sunday celebration instruction sheet

At _____

On _____

Time _____

For more information, contact _____

_____

As part of our Good Shepherd Sunday celebrations, you are invited to make a model sheep, or create a piece of artwork, to bring along to the service. Below are two Bible passages to help you with your ideas. Please bring your finished model or artwork to church with you so that we can include it in a display of all the entries. If you plan to produce a particularly large model, perhaps as part of a group effort, please give us prior notice so we can arrange to give you a suitable space. Refreshments and activities will be available after the service and during the exhibition.

You, Lord, are my shepherd. I will never be in need.
You let me rest in fields of green grass.
You lead me to streams of peaceful water,
and you refresh my life.

You are true to your name,
and you lead me along the right paths.
I may walk through valleys as dark as death,
but I won't be afraid.
You are with me,
and your shepherd's rod makes me feel safe.

You treat me to a feast, while my enemies watch.
You honour me as your guest,
and you fill my cup until it overflows.

Your kindness and love will always be with me
each day of my life,
and I will live forever in your house, Lord.

PSALM 23

I tell you for certain that I am the gate for the sheep. Everyone who came before me was a thief or a robber, and the sheep did not listen to any of them. I am the gate. All who come in through me will be saved. Through me they will come and go and find pasture.

A thief comes only to rob, kill, and destroy. I came so that everyone would have life, and have it in its fullest. I am the good shepherd, and the good shepherd gives up his life for his sheep. Hired workers are not like the shepherd. They don't own the sheep, and when they see a wolf coming, they run off and leave the sheep. Then the wolf attacks and scatters the flock. Hired workers run away because they don't care about the sheep.

I am the good shepherd. I know my sheep, and they know me. Just as the Father knows me, I know the Father, and I give up my life for my sheep. I have other sheep that are not in this sheep pen. I must bring them together too, when they hear my voice. Then there will be one flock of sheep and one shepherd.

JOHN 10:7–16

Visit www.barnabasinchurches.org.uk/extra-resources/ for a free download.

35

Celebrate Good Shepherd Sunday! Poster

At _____

On _____

Time _____

Everyone welcome!

Refreshments and activities

Make and bring your own model sheep

Visit www.barnabasinchurches.org.uk/extra-resources/ for a free download.

36

*

— An activity for summer —

Flower festival

Date: Any time

Web link

www.nafas.org.uk

Introduction

Flower festivals are popular as fund-raising events or to showcase the talents of flower arrangers. The ingenuity of flower arrangers leads many people to marvel, and the best festivals provide displays to illustrate a theme. Done well, these cause visitors to ponder and identify the ideas. Flower festivals are not always particularly of interest to children, and sometimes they do not make the most of the opportunities for evangelism. This suggestion identifies some ideas to engage the interest of children (which means that the adults will then be able to pause and reflect for longer) and ways to encourage everyone to ponder on the things of God.

Key Bible verse

God said, 'I command the earth to produce all kinds of plants, including fruit trees and grain.' And that's what happened. The earth produced all kinds of vegetation. God looked at what he had done and saw that it was good.

GENESIS 1:11–12

Bible links

- Numbers 17:8 (Aaron's stick grows flowers)
- Proverbs 4:8–9 (valuing Wisdom is like wearing a crown of flowers)
- Isaiah 35:2 (deserts will bloom)
- Isaiah 40:8 (flowers fade but what God has said will never change)
- Isaiah 61:3 (the Lord has sent me to give flowers in place of sorrow)
- Isaiah 61:11 (the Lord will give justice like flowers blooming)
- Luke 12:27 (wild flowers grow without effort)
- 1 Corinthians 3:6 (we plant but God makes the seeds sprout and grow)
- James 3:18 (plant seeds of peace to harvest justice)

Key focus: Building community relationships; fun; providing sacred space for reflection; sharing the Christian story

Key group: Church family; schools; local community; families

Activity ideas

Make sure that the overall title chosen for the festival will appeal to people who do not usually go to church. For example, now that few schools teach traditional hymns, the number of people who will have nostalgic memories of singing 'All things bright and beautiful' or 'All creatures of our God and King' is dwindling. This means that a festival entitled 'Hymns in Flowers' will have more limited appeal. A wider audience will be attracted by a theme such as 'Hopes and Dreams' or 'Wonderful World'.

If possible, use a Bible verse as the starting point for each arrangement and display this clearly beside the flowers. It would be good to add an open question below the verse to challenge people in their thinking. For example, an arrangement based on Isaiah 61:3 would portray the changing flow from sorrow to flowers, and an appropriate question might be, 'Which of your sorrows would you like God to replace with flowers?'

Provide one or two places with clear instructions in different parts of the building where people are prompted to pray. For example, based on Isaiah 35:2, set up a large flat container of water. A 60cm plant pot saucer, filled with 2cms depth of water, would be ideal. Supply sheets of coloured paper, pencils and child-safe scissors. Invite people to cut out a small flower shape to be their prayer. They need to bend the petals inwards to meet in the middle. Once they have done this, they can add a written prayer in the centre of the flower if they wish and then they can put the flower into the water. As they watch, the water will cause the petals of the flower to open and bloom.

Another prayer activity would be to provide large, lightweight plastic troughs or tubs filled with compost. Invite people to plant a seed as they pray and point out that the church will continue to pray the prayers that the growing blooms represent in the weeks ahead. A Bible verse to use with this activity might be James 3:18. It is best to choose seeds or corms that are large enough to handle easily, such as anemones. After the festival, move the containers outside so that the seedlings will get the light they need once they have germinated. It might be possible to bring them in for a service for everyone to see the growth they have made.

Make sure also to provide a traditional prayer board, with paper and pens for people to write prayer requests, or a box to post their written needs, as many people accept such an opportunity.

If there is space provide a craft table for anyone who wishes to make a flower.

Provide Plasticine® so that people can sculpt a tiny flower to add to an artificial garden on a tray. Lego® or similar bricks can also be used to make flowers and may appeal more to boys.

A messier idea is to provide coffee filter papers to be painted with water colour paints, or decorated with fibre pens if painting will be too messy. Start by gathering the centre together from the outside and twist a green chenille stick around the gathering to make a stem. Then paint or colour the paper in a bright colour. The flower can be taken home or be added to a drift of flowers laid on green backing paper.

Also offer paper and drawing materials and invite people to design their own flower arrangement to illustrate a given Bible verse.

— Prayer —

God of Creation, we praise you for the beauty of the flowers you have made for us. Thank you for all the people who are working to bring this flower festival together and for all the people, of all ages, who will visit. Paul said that he planted seeds of faith and Apollos watered them before you, Creator God, made them sprout and grow. We pray for the seeds we will plant during the festival. We ask you to send people of faith to water the seeds and we look to see the new shoots you will cause to grow.

Developing the theme

One way to make relationships and build new friendships is to offer flower-arranging sessions both in the run-up to the flower festival and afterwards. A skilled flower arranger will be able to help older children and adults to make a simple arrangement, and it might be possible for them to contribute a small design for a less prominent place. If no one in the church family has the skills to do this, approach the National Association of Flower Arrangers to find a demonstrator.

Another way to do this would be to offer to run a flower-arranging club as a lunchtime or after-school event for a few weeks before the festival. If the club's masterpiece(s) cannot be exhibited at the main festival, perhaps because of timing, take photographs and create a display to showcase the work of the children.

Mission ideas for Autumn
(September, October, November)

*

Cakes for kids

Date: 12–19 September

Web links

www.freecakesforkids.org.uk
www.nationalcupcakeweek.co.uk

Introduction

Many people love baking and eating cake but it can be a somewhat selfish pastime. This idea links with National Cupcake Week to bless the children of the local community with cake.

Key Bible verse

Celebrate by having parties and by giving to the poor and by sharing gifts of food with each other.

ESTHER 9:22B

Bible link

• Nehemiah 8:12 (celebrate by sharing food with those in need)

Key focus: Campaigning and social action

Key group: Church family; local community; families

Activity ideas

Free Cakes for Kids is a voluntary organisation that provides a home-made birthday cake for children who would not otherwise get one. The organisation needs volunteers to bake such cakes, to be a local organiser or to transport cakes between the baker and the receiving family. A church could set up as a local centre if there is not one locally. This would enable them both to bless the children who would receive a cake and to build relationships with people in the community, not necessarily church members, who wish to get involved with baking.

— Prayer —

Wonderful God, thank you for the invention of cake. Sponge or fruit, chocolate or carrot, cake reminds us that all good things come from you. Plentiful and artistic toppings remind us of the extravagance of your creation. Help us to be generous with the gift of cake. Bless those who bake or eat this cake.

Developing the theme

Bless the local community by taking cupcakes, homemade or bought, into local businesses and institutions, such as schools, residential homes and surgeries, to enjoy at their coffee break. Provide a visiting card or similar to accompany each cake to tell people who has provided their cake. This could read: 'A coffee-break treat from… (name of church)'. If appropriate, include the church website address or Facebook page.

* * *

The Big Draw

Date: October

Web links

www.campaignfordrawing.org
www.nadfas.org.uk (click What we do > NADFAS and young people)

Introduction

Since its launch in 2000, The Big Draw has become a month-long festival to encourage people of all ages to draw more. Drawing encourages us to think carefully about the subject matter we are drawing.

Key Bible verse

And he has given them all kinds of artistic skills, including the ability to design and embroider with blue, purple, and red wool and to weave fine linen.

EXODUS 35:35

Bible link

• Job 38:14 (Creation shows God as an artist)

Key focus: Sharing the Christian story; providing sacred space for reflection

Key group: Church family; schools; local community; families

Activity ideas

Hold a drawing festival in church for all ages during half-term week. Provide a range of activities, such as those suggested below.

• Illustrate a verse from a psalm such as Psalm 65
• Sketch a favourite part of the church (suggest some 'tiny' areas as well as the more obvious bigger ones)
• Have a 'trail' of objects and places to find around the church which must then be sketched
• Brass rubbing if you have suitable brasses or can borrow templates

- Calligraphy
- Create an altar-frontal on A2 card to use the following Sunday. Sketch a suitable outline and invite everyone to decorate a small part of it
- Add a self-portrait to a large display of everyone taking part in the event
- Decorate a plain biscuit with ready-to-use tubes of icing

Supply a range of pencils, pastels, paints, pens and papers to encourage everyone to be adventurous in their work. The National Association of Decorative & Fine Arts Societies may be able to provide an artist, through their Young Arts programme, to help children try different techniques.

— Prayer —

Draw around your hand. Add your name to the centre of the hand shape and one word or picture to show your particular prayer request. Use sticky tack to display all the hand prayers. Invite everyone to look at the hands and pray for the requests. Some people may choose to pray by putting their own hand on to each hand prayer.

Developing the theme

Another way to join in The Big Draw is to invite everyone to listen to and then draw a Bible reading at a service. Give everyone a sheet of A4 paper and a pencil. Get them to fold their paper in half twice to make four A6 (postcard) size sections. Beforehand, divide the Bible passage into four parts that make for good stopping points. Start by reading the first section and then, after a pause, invite everyone to draw. Everyone then draws what they just heard in the first part of the story on one quarter of the paper. Emphasise this is a quick draw activity meant to portray the story and not a work of art. As most people finish their drawing, begin reading the second section of the passage. This sequence continues for the remaining three sections until the whole Bible passage has been read and everyone has completed four drawings. In twos or threes compare the illustrations made—not for quality, but to compare what people thought was important in each section of the reading.

* * *

Bible Sunday

Date: Last Sunday after Trinity

Web links

www.davpack.co.uk
www.flickr.com/photos/dioceseofpeterborough/sets/
72157626968651578/show/ (to see a selection of Shoebox Bible verses from Peterborough Diocese)

Introduction

To mark the 400th anniversary of the Authorised Version of the Bible in 2011, Dr Stephen Partridge, Director of Education, Diocese of Peterborough, came up with the astonishing idea of the Shoebox Bible Exhibition in Peterborough Cathedral. Each shoebox contained someone's interpretation of a Bible verse. Nearly 4,000 boxes, covering every book of the Bible, were created and displayed in the correct order. The creativity with which the boxes were made and the deep challenge of the interpretations made many people realise what a valuable exercise this had been. The idea here is a much smaller, and more manageable, version for churches, schools or uniformed groups to try. Flat-packed shoeboxes can be bought from Davpack.

Key Bible verse

Your word is a lamp that gives light wherever I walk.
PSALM 119:105

Bible links

- Matthew 4:4 (Jesus quotes scripture)
- Matthew 13:52 (every student of scripture finds new and old treasure)
- Romans 2:18 (scripture teaches us how to behave)
- Romans 15:4 (scripture encourages us)
- 2 Timothy 3:16–17 (scripture shows us how to live)

Key focus: Sharing the Christian story; providing sacred space for reflection

Key group: Children; church family; schools; local community; families; uniformed groups

Activity ideas

Select a book from the Bible to be the main focus of the final display. Younger children prefer to illustrate concrete things rather than abstract ideas so it would be good to start with a Gospel or one of the Psalms in the first instance. Older children, teenagers and adults may get more of a challenge in finding a visual way to illustrate theological concepts and reflection. If the activity is repeated on another occasion, a book from the Old Testament or one or more of the Epistles could be chosen.

Create a list of each verse in the selected book so that everyone can sign up for the verse they want to illustrate. Have Bibles available so that people can check the content of their verse at this stage. Consider marking some of the verses as particularly suitable for children to interpret. Not all verses will be chosen but this does not matter. It is good to have a sample box or two made in advance so that people can be encouraged to be inventive. If there are plans to create a uniform display, provide identical shoeboxes for everyone to use. These can be specially purchased from a specialist packaging firm. Otherwise most people will be able to find a shoebox at home.

The making of the shoeboxes can be the basis of an all-age session or they can be made at home and brought to the exhibition. Uniformed groups may wish to make them as the main activity at a pack meeting.

— Prayer —

Light of the World, help us to use the Bible to find the light we need for each day's journey. Then show us how to be light for the world where we live. Amen

Developing the theme

Persuading other groups outside the congregation to create shoeboxes is a way of building community links and helping them to engage with the Bible. For example, volunteers could take shoeboxes and craft materials into residential homes to help residents take part. Equally the local school or nursery could be invited to take part.

* * *

Pumpkin party

Date: end of October

Web link

www.bbc.co.uk/food/pumpkin

Introduction

A pumpkin party is a way to provide a wholesome alternative activity to Hallowe'en at the end of October.

Key Bible verse

The fruit of the Spirit is love, joy, peace, forbearance, kindness, goodness, faithfulness, gentleness and self-control.

GALATIANS 5:22–23A (NIV)

Bible links

- Genesis 1:29 (God provides fruit for us to eat)
- Matthew 12:33 (a good tree produces good fruit)

Key focus: Fun

Key group: Church family; schools; local community; families

Activity ideas

The party activities below have been developed from ideas by Nick and Susan Holford of Langham, Rutland. They were inspired to invite their whole village to a party serving a wide range of pumpkin recipes.

Games

- Hunt the pumpkin seeds (hide dried pumpkin seeds around the room as a simple treasure hunt). Younger children will prefer to look for small pumpkin shapes cut out of orange paper.
- Musical pumpkins (dance to the music, freeze in a pumpkin shape when the music stops)

- Pass the hot pumpkin (see 'Hot potato' in games appendix on page 190)
- Pin the stalk on the pumpkin (see 'Pin the tail on the donkey' on page 191)
- Pumpkin pie (see 'Port and starboard' on page 192)
- Sleeping pumpkins (see 'Sleeping lions' on page 192)
- Squash, squash, pumpkin (see 'Duck, duck, goose' on page 190)

Crafts

Older children can help to carve out the name 'Jesus' into the skin of the pumpkin lanterns that have already been hollowed out to make soup and to provide the seeds. Simple star or Christian cross shapes would be easier to carve. When a lit tea light is added, the light for the world shines out. The finished lanterns could be displayed outside the meeting place to share with other people who are out and about.

Younger children can be given a paper plate to create a pretend pumpkin. Paint the underside of the plate orange beforehand and allow it to dry. Invite children to glue yellow letters on to the orange side, spelling out 'Jesus' to look as though the pumpkin is aglow. Glue on two green leaves and a brown stalk, all cut from paper, to complete the design. Miniature versions can be made using the orange screw tops from plastic juice bottles or milk cartons that contained 1 per cent fat skimmed milk.

Refreshments

Make pumpkin soup using the pulp scooped out to create the hollow lanterns for carving.

Roast the pumpkin seeds saved from making the soup. Rinse and pat dry to remove any pulp. Spread on to a baking tray lined with foil. Drizzle with olive oil and a small sprinkle of salt. Roast at 160 degrees or Gas Mark 3 for 10 minutes. Stir to turn and roast for a further 10 minutes, or until golden. For a different flavour, the seeds can be sprinkled with herbs before baking or drizzled with Marmite that has been diluted with a little water.

Pumpkin pie makes a good dessert, and pumpkin puree (with a little cinnamon flavouring) will replace apple puree in muffin recipes.

NB: There is a good selection of pumpkin recipes on the food section of the BBC website.

— Prayer —

For pumpkin pie and pumpkin soup we give you thanks, O Lord.
For pumpkin crafts and pumpkin games we give you praise, O Lord.

Developing the theme

Many older people are anxious about anti-social behaviour at the time of Hallowe'en. Offer to keep them company in the evening. A family could take pumpkin soup and other goodies to share. Equally, many of the party activities could be shared at home inviting just one other family to take part. A lit lantern, placed outside, with 'Jesus' carved out is an important witness that any household can make.

✻ ✻ ✻

All Saints' Day

Date: 1 November

Web link

www.bbc.co.uk/religion/religions/christianity/holydays/allsaints_1.shtml

Introduction

The season of All Saints provides us with an opportunity both to remember and to learn from Christians who served God in the past, and to think about our own call to serve him. Beyond this, how do we encourage people to understand that the Bible can speak directly to us as individuals? One way is to get them to respond as the reading proceeds. The Revised Common Lectionary sets the passage from Ephesians 1 for All Saints' Day in Year C.

Key Bible verse

All of you faithful people, praise our glorious Lord! Celebrate and worship.

PSALM 149:5

Bible links

- Ephesians 1:11–23 (Jesus brings us spiritual blessings)
- Hebrews 3:13 (encourage one another)

Key focus: Providing sacred space for reflection; sharing the Christian story

Key group: Church family; schools; local community; families

Activity ideas

Bible reading

The following reading is based on Ephesians 1:11–23. In preparation, make prompt signs for all the responses that everyone joins in. If there are large numbers of people, there may need to be more than one person holding up prompt signs. Alternatively, use a projected PowerPoint slide for each response. Practise the first four responses before the actual reading so that everyone is ready to take part. Some groups may enjoy singing the 'Hallelujah' response in the way it is scored as the first phrase of the Hallelujah chorus in Handel's *Messiah*.

Leader: God always does what he plans.

Response: Really?

Leader: That's why he appointed Christ to choose us.

Response: Us?

Leader: He did this so that we would bring honour to him and be the first ones to have hope because of him.

Response: He chose us?

Leader: Christ also brought us the truth, which is the good news about how we can be saved.

Response: Hallelujah!

Leader: We put our faith in Christ and were given the promised Holy Spirit to show that we belong to God.

Response: Whoosh!

Leader: The Spirit also makes us sure that we will be given what God has stored up for his people.

Response: Thank you, Lord God.

Leader: Then we will be set free, and God will be honoured and praised.

Response: Hallelujah!

Leader: I have heard about your faith in the Lord Jesus and your love for all of God's people. So I never stop being grateful for you, as I mention you in my prayers.

Response: Double thank you, Lord God!

Leader: I ask the glorious Father and God of our Lord Jesus Christ to give us his Spirit.

Response: Yes, please!

Leader: The Spirit will make us wise and let us understand what it means to know God.

Response: Yes, please!

Leader: My prayer is that light will flood our hearts.

Response: Show us the light.

Leader: And that we will understand the hope that was given to us when God chose us.

Response: Fab!

Leader: Then we will discover the glorious blessings that will be ours together with all of God's people.

Response: Awesome!

Leader: I want you to know about the great and mighty power that God has for us followers. It is the same wonderful power he used when he raised Christ from death and let him sit at his right side in heaven.

Response: Wow!

Leader: There Christ rules over all forces, authorities, powers, and rulers.

Response: Amazing!

Leader: He rules over all beings in this world and will rule in the future world as well.

Response: More than... (add name of someone that young people might think of as powerful)

Leader: God has put all things under the power of Christ, and for the good of the church he has made him the head of everything.

Response: Jesus is the King.
Leader: The church is Christ's body.
Response: You mean us?
Leader: And is filled with Christ who completely fills
               everything.
Response: Hallelujah! Thank you, Lord God.

Song idea

'Come all you people, come and praise your maker'

Craft idea

Provide everyone with three linked paper dolls (these can be cut out beforehand). Invite people to make the central doll into a self-portrait as a 'saint-in-training'. Then decorate one of the other dolls to represent someone who has been important to them on their Christian journey (it may be necessary to make some suggestions such as a godparent, a teacher, a minister, a friend and so on). Finally ask them to use the third doll to represent someone who has been a saint who inspired people in the past. This third doll could show recent 'saints' like Martin Luther King and Mother Teresa, or more distant people from history including biblical characters. People can either take their linked 'saints' home as a reminder or glue them, with everyone else's, to a large sheet of coloured paper or card to create a big display.

— Prayer —

If the following prayer is to be used in a church, invite everyone to join hands in a circle right round the building or meeting space. Ask them to imagine some of the many people who have prayed in there in the past.

All-powerful and ever-living God, we rejoice as we remember so many people who have had faith in you across the centuries. It is awesome, exciting and inspiring to realise that we stand in line with them to worship you. Hallelujah, we praise your holy name.

Developing the theme

Invite everyone to write an email or postcard to someone who has influenced their Christian life. Thanking people, especially if they are unaware of the influence they have made, is powerful. Everyone needs encouragement and the Bible tells us to do just that (Hebrews 3:13).

* * *

Remembrance and St Martin's Day

Date: 11 November

Web link

www.ukgermanconnection.org

Introduction

The renewal of interest in Remembrance Day gives churches many opportunities. Uniformed organisations may wish to attend a Sunday service of Remembrance or invite someone to lead activities at a group meeting. Schools may welcome someone to lead collective worship on or around 11 November or to contribute to an RE lesson. St Martin, whose feast is celebrated on 11 November, is the patron saint of soldiers and makes a good focus for the occasion.

Key Bible verse

When I was hungry, you gave me something to eat, and when I was thirsty, you gave me something to drink. When I was a stranger, you welcomed me, and when I was naked, you gave me clothes to wear. When I was sick, you took care of me, and when I was in jail, you visited me.

MATTHEW 25:35–36

Bible link

• 1 Timothy 6:12 (fight a good fight to claim eternal life)

Key focus: Building community relationships; providing sacred space for reflection

Key group: Church family; schools; local community; families; uniformed groups

Activity ideas

Explain that St Martin was a soldier in the Roman army around AD330 even though he was not yet 18 years old. Invite someone to act the part of St Martin. Provide them with a sword and a cloak to drape round their shoulders. The cloak should be made in two parts so that it can be divided. (It is possible to use two lengths of brown crêpe paper lightly linked together at the top shoulders for this or two lengths of fabric joined with some press studs or Velcro®). Ask them to act being an important soldier marching around. Then ask someone else to take the part of a poor beggar shivering at the side of the road because the weather was so cold. St Martin sees the beggar and immediately takes off his cloak, divides it into two and gives one half to the beggar. The beggar wraps their share of the cloak round them and St Martin walks away trying to pull the cloak round him and now shivering slightly.

At Remembrance time, we think of the sacrifice that so many service personnel have made in times of war. Hundreds of thousands of people have given their lives in the cause of freedom. Many, many more have given years of their lives to serve the good of other people. Few, if any of us, will be called to sacrifice our lives. However, we can all make sure that we try to share what we have and to serve the needs of other people just like St Martin the soldier.

— Prayer —

Give everyone a small sheet of paper. Invite them to imagine the paper represents all their clothes or toys or money (depending on the age group). Explain that halfway through the prayer you will ask them to tear their paper into two when you tear your own sheet.

Sovereign Lord, we thank you for the life and example of St Martin. Inspire us to work for freedom and justice. Help us to share our possessions (**tear paper**) *with those in need and to protect those who are at risk in any way.*

Arrange to collect up the 'other half' of the sheets so that they have been given away symbolically.

Developing the theme

There is a tradition in Flanders, parts of the Netherlands, Germany and Austria to hold lantern processions in the evening of St Martin's Day. Hold an activity session to think about the story of St Martin and to make paper lanterns. There are simple instructions on the website of UK–German Connection using tea light candles, cheese boxes and transparent paper. It is also traditional to eat *Weckmann*, a sweet bread loaf in the shape of a man with raisins for eyes. It would be possible for those attending the activity session to start by shaping their *Weckmann* out of dough that has already been mixed before the start of the session. Then the bread could be baked during the other activities so it is ready to be enjoyed after the procession, along with hot chocolate. Plan a short procession outside after dark so that everyone can use their lantern. Arrange for some adults who are not directly responsible for children to lead and follow the procession. These adults should wear high-visibility clothing and carry torches, rather than a lantern, to ensure safety.

✳ ✳ ✳

No music day and St Cecilia's Day

Date: 21 and 22 November

Web link

www.nomusicday.com

Introduction

St Cecilia is the patron saint of musicians because she is reported to have sung to God as she died. This idea encourages people to consider music as a gift by observing a day of 'no music' followed by a day of making music.

Key Bible verses

Sing a new song. Shout! Play beautiful music.
PSALM 33:3

You silence the roaring waves and the noisy shouts of the nations.
PSALM 65:7

Bible links

- 2 Samuel 6:5 (David and others made music and danced before the Lord)
- Psalm 57:7 (I will make music for God)
- Habakkuk 2:20 (Let the world be silent, the Lord is present)

Key focus: Fun; providing sacred space for reflection

Key group: Church family; families; schools; uniformed groups

Activity ideas

This is a two-part activity. Challenge everyone to avoid listening to music as far as possible on 21 November. This means not using the radio, personal music players and so on. (You may need to make allowances for times when it is not possible to avoid music, such as during the school day if it is played during assembly. Equally, as most shops provide music it may be hard to avoid it on a shopping trip, although people may decide not to visit a shopping mall that day in order to meet this part of the challenge fully.) Decide beforehand about watching television, seeing that most programmes include background music. Use some of the non-music time to decide what music to play at particular points during the following day. Also plan time to be still and silent; make time to listen to God.

Then, the next day, plan to enjoy as much music as possible. Start by playing a track that will encourage everyone to 'sing to God' as they get ready for their day. Choose praise music to listen to on the way to school or work, and something quieter and more reflective for lunchtime. Plan to eat a family meal without conversation but listening to music that sings to God—ask everyone for their suggestion to add to the playlist. Choose a hymn or worship song to sing together at the end of the day.

— Prayer —

Sing:

> *Praise God from whom all blessings flow,*
> *Praise him, all creatures here below,*
> *Praise him above, you heavenly host,*
> *Praise Father, Son and Holy Ghost.*
>
> THOMAS KEN, 1637–1711

Developing the theme

Search on YouTube for a hymn or worship song that has been illustrated with visuals. Start by searching for 'Be Still and Know' as that will capture something about the silence and listening of this idea.

* * *

St Andrew's Day

Date: 30 November

Web links

www.st-andrew.org.uk/standrew.htm
www.scotland.org/culture/festivals/st-andrews-day/the-story-of-st-andrew (an animated version of the life and legend of St Andrew)

Introduction

Many churches are dedicated to St Andrew, and he has been the patron saint of Scotland since the mid-tenth century. The life of St Andrew, and the different ways he is remembered across the world, provides plenty of material for an activity session. Invite people from the local community to share in celebrations for the patronal festival or for Scotland's special day.

Key Bible verse

The first thing Andrew did was to find his brother and tell him, 'We have found the Messiah!'

JOHN 1:41

Bible links

- Matthew 4:18–21 (Jesus chooses four fishermen)
- Matthew 10:2 (Andrew was an apostle)
- John 1:42 (Andrew brings his brother to Jesus)
- John 6:1–14 (Jesus feeds 5,000 people)
- Acts 1:6–11 (Andrew was there when Jesus was taken up into heaven)
- Acts 1:12–14 (Andrew gathered with all the disciples to pray)

Key focus: Fun; providing a sacred space for reflection; sharing the Christian story

Key group: Church family; schools; local community; families

Activity ideas

Gathering activity

Attach a large sheet of paper to a wall or board. Put the name ANDREW in the centre with its meaning ('man' or 'warrior') underneath. As each person arrives, add their first name. Then use a book that explains the significance of first names to identify the meaning of everyone's name. Chat about why our parents may have chosen our name.

Introduction

Today's event will look at the life of Andrew: the first disciple of Jesus, an apostle and now remembered as a saint, a holy person of God. The Bible tells us that Andrew was always keen to bring other people to Jesus. He was a 'networker' and these days might have been a keen user of Facebook or Twitter.

Network challenge

Find someone you have not met before or do not know very well, ask their name and find out something about them. Keep in a pair with that person and find another pair. Then share what you have discovered about your partner with the two new people. Once all four people have shared something, meet up with another four to share eight bits of information.

Games

Andrew was good at passing on the message of the good news of Jesus. Play 'Telephone' (also known as 'Chinese whispers'). The game can be found on page 193.

A much noisier 'message' game is 'Megaphone' in which two opposing teams attempt to share a Bible verse. Suitable Bible verses to use include: Genesis 1:1; Joshua 1:9; Psalm 23; Psalm 46:10a; Psalm 119:105; John 1:1; John 14:6. The game can be found on page 191.

Play 'pass the parcel' with one individual word from John 1:41 hidden in each layer. Make sure the words are jumbled before wrapping or someone will soon spot that they are in order. Once all the layers have been unwrapped, the challenge is to sort them into the correct order. If the numbers attending the event are large, make up more than one parcel to be unwrapped by two or more groups to help younger children maintain interest.

Craft

Create a huge mural to show the key moments of St Andrew's life. Allocate a different episode to each mixed-age group so that they can work independently on a standard sheet of backing paper that will match up with all the others. The main incidents to illustrate might be:

1. Andrew and another man with John the Baptist meeting Jesus and calling him 'Rabbi', which means teacher (John 1:35-39).
2. Andrew fetching his brother, Simon, to meet Jesus (John 1:40–42).
3. Andrew fishing alongside Simon when Jesus invites them to join him (Mark 1:16–20).
4. Andrew is one of the twelve disciples Jesus sends out to heal people (Matthew 10:1–4).
5. Andrew finds a boy who is willing to share his lunch with Jesus and the crowd (John 6:8–9).
6. Andrew was there when Jesus was taken up into heaven (Acts 1:6–11).
7. Andrew gathered with all the disciples to pray in the upper room (Acts 1:12–14).

Provide a range of craft materials such as cellophane paper, corrugated card or bubblewrap to create a rugged landscape; shades of green, brown and blue tissue and crêpe paper, and different materials to turn into people as well as a range of glues and sticky tack and tape.

Refreshments

It would be fun to include different dishes from the many places in the world that celebrate Andrew as a special saint, particularly if there are plenty of adults present. Children may prefer more simple food.

- Scotland: shortbread, Black Bun (fruitcake cased in pastry), oatcakes, haggis
- Greece: moussaka, olives, baklava, halva
- Russia: dill pickles, blini served with sour cream
- Sicily: pasta
- Ukraine: dumplings, potato pancakes

— Prayer —

Amazing God, thank you for Andrew's enthusiasm for bringing people to Jesus. Give us the courage and eagerness to do the same. May we find knowing Jesus so exciting that we are passionate about sharing his good news with everyone.

Developing the theme

St Andrew was a 'networker'. Encourage a group of people to develop a Facebook page to talk about the St Andrew's Day events in your area and to locate other pages linked to St Andrew.

Mission ideas for Winter
(December, January and February)

✳

National Tree Week

Date: late November or early December

Web links

www.kidsclosertonature.co.uk
www.treecouncil.org.uk/community-action/national-tree-week
www.treesforcities.org
www.woodlandtrust.org.uk

Introduction

Trees often symbolise life and spiritual health in the Bible. National Tree Week provides an opportunity to encourage people to enjoy trees in the local area and to think about planting at least one.

Key Bible verse

Good people will prosper like palm trees, and they will grow strong like the cedars of Lebanon.

PSALM 92:12

Bible links

- Psalm 1:3 (God's people are like healthy, fruitful trees)
- Psalm 52:8 (olive trees in the house of God)
- Psalm 92:12 (good people prosper like palm trees)
- Luke 6:43–45 (a tree and its fruit)
- Romans 11:16b (good roots are important)

Key focus: Building community relationships; fun; fund-raising for charity

Key group: Church family; families; local community; schools; uniformed groups

Activity ideas

National Tree Week encourages everyone to become more aware of trees. Organise a Tree Walk to find and identify trees locally. Even urban areas will have some trees to be found, although prior research may be necessary to ensure that the Tree Walk will be successful. Borrow a simple tree book from the library so that specimens can be identified if no one has the necessary knowledge. Collect any fallen twigs or leaves that are on the ground to use later on.

Follow the walk with an hour for activities and refreshments. Offer 'tree' themed food and drink such as Twiglets®; vanilla ice cream with maple syrup topping; fig rolls; pieces of apple, pear and banana; hot blackcurrant drink with a squeeze of lemon juice, sprinkle of ground ginger and stirred with a cinnamon stick. Nuts come from trees but it would be best not to offer these because of the risk from nut allergies.

Provide simple activities such as the following ideas.

Palm trees

Tightly roll up a sheet of newspaper along the short side to make a long tube. Seal the open edge with sticky tape. Use scissors to cut about halfway down the tube several times to create fronds. Tease out the separate strands to represent the branches.

Twig trees

Use the fallen twigs collected earlier to make a twig tree (or tower). Create a triangular base from the largest twigs and keep building it up until all the twigs have been used, or until it falls down.

Christmas trees

Together, make a large 3-D Christmas tree from cardboard boxes. Encourage everyone to keep standing back to check the overall shape during construction. If the space of the venue allows, spray the tree green once it is finished. The tree could be kept in church over the Christmas season. Alternatively, consider organising the event through a library and then the artwork could be left on display there.

Prayer trees

Display a large bare branch and ask people to tie paper leaves on to which their prayer requests have been written to the branch. Alternatively, draw an outline on a large sheet of paper on to which the paper leaves can be glued.

Tree decorations

Make a simple Christmas tree decoration such as decorating a star shape with glitter and adding some wool as a tie. This will serve as a reminder of the event when added to home Christmas trees. A set of stickers could be printed so that each person's star can have the words of Psalm 52:8 or Psalm 92:12 stuck on to the reverse.

Prayer leaves

At the end of the session, invite everyone to take a small pinch of heart-shaped confetti (to represent God's love) and challenge them to carry it home balanced on one of the fallen leaves gathered during the walk.

Prayer

Creator God, may we be like healthy trees, deeply rooted in you and reaching down to drink the living water of Jesus; growing green leaves as we mature in Christ and producing the good fruits of your Holy Spirit to build up life in our community (based on Psalm 1:3).

Developing the theme

Raise money at the Tree Walk event to buy some trees to plant locally if there is a suitable site. Of course, if you are based in an urban area, there may be few opportunities to plant a tree. In this instance, fund-raise to donate and dedicate a tree through the Woodland Trust or Trees for Cities.

* * *

Knitted Christmas tree

Date: throughout December

Web link

www.oxfam.org.uk

Introduction

The origin of this brilliant idea is not clear, but the beauty of the project is that it does two things at once. The initial undertaking is to invite people to create a knitted Christmas tree to display in church or another local public space and thus develop community relationships. Then, after the Christmas season, the knitted squares can take on a second life for charity.

Key Bible verse

I provided clothes for the poor, and I was praised for supplying woollen garments to keep them warm.

JOB 31:19–20

Bible links

- 2 Chronicles 3:14 (wool used to decorate Solomon's temple)
- Matthew 25:37–40 (providing clothes for the needy is like clothing the king)

Key focus: Building community relationships; campaigning and social action; fun; fund-raising for charity

Key group: Church family; families; local community; schools; uniformed groups

Activity ideas

Issue a community challenge to get as many people as possible to knit a 20cm (8 inch) square from green wool to reach a total of at least a thousand squares. The squares can then be mounted on to a metal conical frame to create a Christmas tree. The tree will look particularly effective if varying shades of green wool are used. It is a good idea to make a mini tree beforehand, which can then be photographed, so that people can get some idea of the nature of the project. Search on-line for 'knitted Christmas tree' to see what other projects have looked like.

Approach uniformed groups and residential homes to see if they will take part in the challenge. It may be necessary to provide them with wool and needles—these can often be found cheaply in charity shops or by asking members of the church family if they have any to spare. Provide a sheet of instructions so that all the squares are the same size and knitted in garter stitch. This sheet should also give the closing date for the squares to be handed in and could include the photograph of the mini tree for inspiration. It may also be possible to offer to run a 'learn-to-knit' lunchtime or after-school club if there are two keen knitters available to do this. Allow four sessions to cover teaching the basics and to allow time to make a couple of squares. Try to resist the urge to knit 'for' the children but help them to complete their own work, however untidy (in the final display imperfections are unlikely to show up).

Basic knitted square

Using a 50g ball of double knit wool and size 9 (5.5mm) needles, cast on three stitches. Work in garter stitch (every row plain) as follows.

- First row: Knit.
- Second row: Knit one into front and back of first stitch, knit to last stitch, knit one into front and back of last stitch (five stitches).
- Repeat these two rows 22 times more (49 stitches).
- Next row: Knit.
- Next row: Knit two together, knit to last two stitches, knit two together (47 stitches).
- Repeat the last two rows 22 times more (three stitches).
- Next row: cast off remaining three stitches.

Alternatively, a simpler method for beginners would be to cast on 50 stitches and then knit up to 50 rows (or until the knitting is 'square' depending on the tension of the stitches) before casting off. This method will not have the firmness of a square knitted with diagonal rows and pulls out of shape more easily.

— Prayer —

Wonderful God, creator of trees and sheep and human ingenuity, thank you! Thank you that we can use wool to knit simple squares. Thank you that our simple crafts can create an amazing decoration to celebrate the birth of your son, Jesus. From all our fun, we pray that the squares we have knitted can be used in blankets to bring warmth and comfort to those who need them.

Developing the theme

Christmas trees always look better with decorations! Competent knitters will enjoy the challenge of knitting these. Search online for 'mini knitted Christian Christmas decorations' to find patterns for stars and small nativity figures. Once the squares from the main tree have been turned into blankets and sent to charity, the ornaments can either be saved for reuse another year or stored and then sold in aid of a good cause the following autumn.

* * *

St Nicholas' Day

Date: 6 December (or nearest Sunday)

Web link

www.stnicholascenter.org

Introduction

For many people, St Nicholas is the person who has become known as Santa Claus and even Father Christmas. Many families will take children to visit Father Christmas in a shopping or garden centre. This is an idea to welcome families to meet Father Christmas (St Nicholas) in church and to find out about a man who devoted his life to serving Jesus.

Key Bible verse

Give the money to the poor, and you will have riches in heaven.
MATTHEW 19:21

Bible link

* Acts 20:35 (more blessings come from giving than receiving)

Key focus: Fun; providing sacred space for reflection

Key group: Children; church family; families; schools; uniformed groups

Activity ideas

Invite families to meet Father Christmas at a St Nicholas' Day event. Arrange this either as an all-age event or, with consent forms, as a session for unaccompanied children. The latter would allow parents to get on with Christmas preparations if held at the weekend. It could also form the basis of an all-age service. Ensure that a picture of Father Christmas is included on all the publicity. Further information about running an event for unaccompanied children is included in the FAQ section, on page 12.

Gathering activity

Invite everyone to make a bishop's mitre. Instructions can be found at: www.stnicholascenter.org/pages/folding-miters (by kind permission of St Nicholas Center).

Story

Tell the story of St Nicholas using 'pass the parcel' to reveal symbols to illustrate the story. This list of symbols is in reverse order (so that the first listed forms the centre of the parcel and the last on the list is the symbol that is required first in the story).

You will need three socks or shoes; picture of a bishop's mitre; a bag of chocolate coins; a small Bible; a picture of an unhappy face; map of Europe showing Turkey; a bag of chocolate coins.

If possible, invite everyone to sit in a circle. If this is not possible, ask someone to supervise the passing of the parcel along the rows.

The first layer is unwrapped to reveal a bag of chocolate coins.

Leader: Nicholas was born into a very wealthy family.

The second layer is unwrapped to reveal a map of Europe showing Turkey.

Leader: He lived in the village of Patara on the south coast of Turkey.

The third layer is unwrapped to reveal a picture of an unhappy face.

Leader: Nicholas' parents died when he was young.

The fourth layer is unwrapped to reveal a small Bible.

Leader: Nicholas was brought up to believe in God and he tried to live a Christian life.

The fifth layer is unwrapped to reveal more chocolate coins.

Leader: He used all the money he had inherited from his parents to look after people who lived in poverty or were in need.

The sixth layer is unwrapped to reveal a picture of a mitre.

Leader: Other people saw the way he lived his life and Nicholas was made Bishop of Myra.

The seventh layer is unwrapped to reveal three socks or shoes.

Leader: One story told about Nicholas was that he heard
           about a family who could not afford to pay a
           dowry to enable their three daughters to get
           married. One night Nicholas passed their window
           and threw in three bags of gold coins. (Another
           version has Nicholas throwing the coins down
           the chimney.) The coins landed in the shoes of
           the young women. There was enough money so
           they could get married. Many people think that is
           the first time we hear about Santa Claus, which is
           another way of saying St Nicholas, or even Father
           Christmas.

Craft

Make a model St Nicholas to take home using a cardboard tube as
the main base. There are plenty of ideas and instructions on the St
Nicholas Center website. If everyone makes two such models, the
second could be filled with a few chocolate coins and used as a gift
to share the story of St Nicholas with a neighbour, friend or work
colleague.

Game

Invite everyone to take off their shoes and to line them up as if
outside their bedroom door. In church, shoes should be lined up at
the end of the row or pew. Play a round or two of 'sleeping children',
which is played in the same way as 'sleeping lions' (p. 192). While
everyone is pretending to sleep, put a foil-covered chocolate coin in
each pair of shoes (or in each shoe if there are sufficient chocolates)
to be discovered at the end of the game when everyone puts their
shoes back on.

Song (to the tune of 'O Christmas Tree' or 'O Tannenbaum')

St Nicholas, St Nicholas
You were a good and holy man
St Nicholas, St Nicholas
You lived your life to Jesus' plan
You followed Jesus all your days
You used your wealth to give him praise
St Nicholas, St Nicholas
We thank the Lord for Nicholas

St Nicholas, St Nicholas
The world remembers what you did
St Nicholas, St Nicholas
With women married, children fed
May we be generous like you
May we all follow Jesus too
St Nicholas, St Nicholas
We thank the Lord for Nicholas

There is a further selection of songs for use on St Nicholas' Day on the St Nicholas Center website. Most of the songs are set to familiar tunes.

Closing activity

Have a visit from St Nicholas (who may look remarkably like Father Christmas to our eyes) to ask everyone to help other people as they prepare for Christmas.

Prayer

Create a mock chimney. Invite everyone to write or draw a prayer on to an A4 sheet of paper. This is then screwed up into a tight ball and has to be tossed into the chimney. Small children will need to stand close to the receptacle, but older children and adults can be challenged to stand some distance away so they may need more than one throw to make their prayer.

Developing the theme

The activity ideas could be offered as a one-off lunchtime or after-school club. Where schools offer a commercial after-school facility, you could offer to provide an hour's programme for them.

The ideas could also be the basis of a Toy Service with St Nicholas arriving at the end to collect toys that have been donated for distribution to hospitals, women's refuges and via Food Banks.

* * *

Christingle in the community

Date: Anytime in December

Web link

www.childrenssociety.org.uk/christingle

Introduction

Many churches, schools and uniformed groups raise money for The Children's Society by holding Christingle events. This idea encourages people to turn the whole area into a giant Christingle and to pray for different groups of people in the community.

Key Bible verse

The Scriptures say, 'God commanded light to shine in the dark.' Now God is shining in our hearts to let you know that his glory is seen in Jesus Christ.

2 CORINTHIANS 4:6

Bible links

- Matthew 5:14 (We are like light for the world)
- John 3:19 (The light has come into the world)
- John 8:12 (Jesus is light for the world)
- Philippians 2:15 (Shine like lights among people in the world)

Key focus: Fund-raising for The Children's Society; providing sacred space for reflection

Key group: Church family; families; local community; schools; uniformed groups

Activity ideas

You will need to visit the four places where the gifts will be celebrated beforehand to explain what you plan to do and, if necessary, to ask permission. Those who live in a residential home may want to join the group to sing a carol if they have prior notice so that they can assemble ready for the visit. Try to plan a circular route.

Invite everyone to gather at a central meeting place. This could be the church, or a landmark in the centre of the area such as a war memorial, or outside a library or school.

Give everyone a red sticker to wear. Explain that everyone is called to share God's love around the world and the sticker is a symbol of this. The Children's Society often produces Christingle stickers so these could be used instead.

Carry official Children's Society collecting tins for donations during the event.

Light a large candle (although it may not be possible to keep this alight during the prayer walk). Pray for the work of The Children's Society and for insight into the needs of the local community as you walk.

Equip four to six children with red chalk and ask them to take turns to mark the pavement with a chalk heart at regular intervals as the group walks around. This leaves a lasting, but not permanent, reminder of God's love stretching around the community.

Visit four places to celebrate the gifts that people share there. These could be the gift of care at a residential home, the gift of joy in a nursery or playground, the gift of hospitality at a café, the gift of healing at a surgery or pharmacy, or the gift of service in a shop. At each stop light a real Christingle, say a brief prayer for all who live or work there, sing a carol and leave the Christingle as a reminder of the visit.

Continue marking the red ribbon of chalk hearts between each of the stops.

Between the stops to celebrate gifts in the community, also find four places to pause to pray for children in danger of exclusion (outside a school); children who run away (at a bus stop or railway station); children in trouble with the law (outside a police station or by a CCTV camera); children who are refugees (at an area of wasteland, or in a park).

Finally return to the starting point, relight the large candle if necessary, and remind everyone that they have brought God's light into the area by their walk of witness, pray for his blessing on the area and sing a final carol of celebration.

— Prayer —

Jesus, light of the world, we thank you for everyone who works to bring light into our community. We pray for the dark corners. Where do you want us to bring your light? Thank you for the work of The Children's Society. We ask you to bless all the children in their care at this time.

Developing the theme

This activity could also be undertaken by a family, a uniformed organisation, a home group or church children's group as part of their usual session.

* * *

Christingle club

Date: During the four weeks running up to Christmas

Web link

www.childrenssociety.org.uk/christingle

Introduction

Christmas activity clubs are popular. This idea for a club includes four sessions to highlight the different elements of a Christingle. It could be run as a lunchtime or after-school club, as an all-day activity session, or included in meetings of uniformed groups or other church-based clubs. Omit the game or the song if you have only a short time together. Use the craft where it is included in each session as something for the children to take home as they will not receive their completed Christingle until the last meeting.

Key Bible verse

The Scriptures say, 'God commanded light to shine in the dark.' Now God is shining in our hearts to let you know that his glory is seen in Jesus Christ.

2 CORINTHIANS 4:6

Bible links

- Genesis 1:1 (God made the world)
- John 3:16 (God loves the world)
- John 8:12 (Jesus is the light for the world)

Key focus: Fun; providing sacred space for reflection; sharing the Christian story

Key group: Children; church family; schools; uniformed groups

Activity ideas

Session 1: the world (orange)

This session focuses on the world as God's creation.

You will need an orange; paper plates; shallow containers of washable paints; hand wipes; fibre pens (if needed); disposable painting aprons; an inflatable (beach ball-style) globe.

Bible verse

In the beginning God created the heavens and the earth.
GENESIS 1:1

Gather

Show the orange and explain that in a Christingle the orange represents the world. People of the Christian, Jewish and Muslim faiths all believe that God created the world. Ask what people think are the most amazing bits of God's creation and, if necessary, encourage them to think of sunsets and rainbows, waterfalls and waves, butterflies and babies… God created all these wonderful things.

Craft

Provide a plain paper plate for each person. Provide shallow containers of washable paint (plus wipes!) so that everyone can create their own version of the world by finger-painting. If this will be too messy, provide fibre pens, but this is not such fun.

Game

Take it in turns for someone to call out 'God created...' and then everyone has to make a body shape to illustrate what was called out. Be ready to pose as a dinosaur, butterfly, thunder clap or whatever amazing part of creation is thought of.

Song

'He's got the whole world in his hands'

Throw the inflatable globe to each other during the chorus.

— Prayer —

Creator God, thank you for the amazing world you have made for us to enjoy. Help us to look after it and not take more than our share. Please help us to remember other people around the world as we prepare for Christmas.

Session 2: God's love (red band)

In this session the focus is on God's love for the world he made.

You will need an orange; red tape (available from the Children's Society); a very long length of red nylon rope (usually to be found in pound shops) unravelled and rolled into a huge ball; lengths of red wool.

Gather

Invite everyone to help with unrolling the red rope around the edge of the room. Point out that everyone is now on the inside.

Bible verse

God loved the people of this world so much that he gave his only Son.

JOHN 3:16

Discuss

Show the orange and add the red tape to demonstrate God's love in Jesus going right round the world.

Craft

Make friendship bracelets by plaiting three lengths of red wool together.

Game

Invite everyone to think of something they really love. Then go round the group saying, 'God loves me more than (add what they thought of).' For example, responses might be: 'God loves me more than hot chocolate with marshmallows' or 'God loves me more than being at the beach on a sunny day.'

Song

'Jesus' love is very wonderful'

Encourage everyone to do the actions as you sing: stretch up for 'so high', reach down for 'so low', stretch wide for 'so wide'.

— Prayer —

Amazing God, thank you that you love us so much that you gave us your son, Jesus. We are looking forward to Christmas when we celebrate Jesus being born. Help us to remember that your love is for everyone.

Session 3: the fruits (sticks with sweets)

The third session invites everyone to identify the gifts that God gives us.

You will need an orange with pips; a plate; a knife; antibacterial wipes (if needed); cocktail sticks; a selection of small soft sweets and dried fruit; small sandwich bags, sticky labels for each person's name and pens; three sets of postcards as explained in the game description.

Gather

Show the orange and ask the group to guess how many pips it will contain. As you peel the orange, talk about the pips being able to grow into a mature orange tree that produces fruit of its own.

Bible verse

(God's people) are like trees growing beside a stream, trees that produce fruit in season and always have leaves.
PSALM 1:3

Discuss

If the Bible says we should be like healthy trees, what good fruit does God want us to produce for other people?

Craft

Encourage everyone to wash their hands (or use antibacterial wipes). Invite everyone to load four cocktail sticks with sweets and dried fruit and place them into a labelled sandwich bag ready for the next session. Allow sufficient supplies so that some can be eaten during the activity.

NB: if you are working with unaccompanied children, make sure that consent forms for the event include a question about allergies as some children may not be able to eat sweets. In this instance provide a range of dried or crystallised fruits.

Game

Invite three children to form a human 'fruit machine'. Sit them on chairs side-by-side. Give each of them an identical set of three A5 cards. One card should have the symbol of a large heart (love), one a red cross (caring) and one a lemon. The rest of the group take it in turns to pretend to press down the arm of the fruit machine shouting 'go' as they do so. The three children on the chairs then have to select one of their cards (without consulting each other) and hold them up for the group to see. If they all show the same card at the same time, the group has to make a group hug (if all three cards show the heart symbol) or rush round the room (if all the cards show the red cross) or boo loudly (if all the cards show the lemon). Each time a matching set of cards has triggered an activity, three different children take a turn as part of the fruit machine. When the cards do not match, then the group just shouts out 'no' and the next child pretends to press down the arm and so on.

Song

'Harvest hymn'

— Prayer —

Show an example of one of the cocktail sticks loaded with fruit and sweets and then ask everyone to stand on one leg as you pray the following prayer.

Creator God, help us to remember that you want us to produce good fruit for other people. This week we pray that we will be kind and caring and generous and loving—just like Jesus.

Session 4: the light of Jesus (candle)

The final session looks at Jesus coming as the light of the world.

You will need antibacterial wipes (if needed); an orange for each person; red tape (available from The Children's Society); plastic bags of sweets on sticks prepared at the previous session; finger candles; sharp knife for an adult to cut a small cross in the top of each orange; 75mm squares of foil (to catch the candle wax).

Gather

Provide several items that can give light such as a light bulb, a torch, a candle, a glow stick and ask everyone to identify the link between them. (They all provide light but all need to be switched on or lit in some way).

Bible verse

Jesus said, 'I am the light for the world! Follow me, and you won't be walking in the dark.'
JOHN 8:12

Discuss

How does Jesus provide light for the world? Ask for suggestions. If necessary add that Jesus shows us a good way to live so that we can bring his light into the world. Jesus can give us the spark of his love to share with everyone through the power of the Holy Spirit.

Craft

Encourage everyone to wash their hands (or use antibacterial wipes). Fasten red sticky tape around each orange. After a cross has been cut in the top of the orange, lay the square of foil on top and wedge the candle through it and down into the fruit. Add the four cocktail sticks loaded with sweets that were made at the previous session.

Game

Invite everyone to make a body shape to illustrate the different elements of a Christingle as they are called out. Take a few moments for everyone to develop ideas for 'orange', 'red band', 'candle' and 'fruit sticks' before demonstrating a movement for the whole Christingle, such as crouching down in a small ball and then springing up quickly flinging arms up into the air to represent the energy of life. Then call out the different elements in turn to get everyone moving and repeat several times in a different order.

Song

'The Christingle begins with an orange' (tune: 'Sing Hosanna')

Download the song from The Children's Society's website: www. childrenssociety.org.uk/sites/default/files/tcs/the_christingle_ song_0.pdf

— Prayer —

Invite everyone to stand in a circle holding their Christingle. Light the individual Christingles and then pray the following prayers.

Almighty God, thank you for making the amazing world and all the incredible things in it. Thank you for sending your son, Jesus, to be the light for the world. Help us to share his love with everyone we meet.

We pray for the work of the Children's Society. We pray for the staff and volunteers who provide care for the children and young people who need it. We pray for the people who raise money for the Society's work and campaigns. But especially, loving God, we pray for the children and young people who need the help and support the Society provides.

Developing the theme

If the four sessions are offered on the same day each person could build up their own Christingle as part of each activity. Obviously oranges will go soft and the sweets and dried fruit will become stale over three weeks, so it is best then to provide the 'real' Christingle materials during the final meeting to ensure that everything is fresh.

A shorter, edited version could be used with preschool children or with the residents of care homes.

Christingle events are usually used to raise money for The Children's Society. It may be possible to make a small charge for those attending the club or activity session if you make it clear that all money received will go to The Children's Society. Otherwise, give everyone a tube of Smarties® at the end of the first session and encourage them to fill the empty tubes with small coins to be collected together at the fourth gathering.

✳ ✳ ✳

Christmas sketch

Date: Christmas Day

Introduction

Many people think of Jesus as a baby because they come to church only at Christmas and hear the nativity story. This sketch, by Nicholas Orme, makes a strong link between Christmas and Easter, between the nativity and the resurrection.

Key Bible verse

All at once an angel came down to them from the Lord, and the brightness of the Lord's glory flashed around them.
LUKE 2:9

Bible links

- Matthew 28:1–7 (the angel's Easter message)
- Mark 16:1–7 (the angel's Easter message)
- Luke 2:9–17 (the angel's Christmas message)
- Luke 24:1–7 (the angel's Easter message)

Key focus: Sharing the Christian story

Key group: Church family; schools; uniformed groups

Activity ideas

Cast

Sergeant angel; trainee angel; angel Gabriel

Sergeant angel:	Right, lass. Are you up for getting your angel's wings, then? You've done your flying hours. You've passed your flying test. Now all you've got to do is get through the theory test.
Trainee angel:	Yes, sir.
Sergeant angel:	Now just suppose I put you on angel duty on Christmas night. What do you tell everyone?
Trainee angel:	Christ is risen.
Sergeant angel:	Christ is risen? Christ is risen? Haven't you done any homework? Christ is born. Go on from there, 'Today in the city of…
Trainee angel:	Jerusalem.
Sergeant angel:	Not Jerusalem. Bethlehem. That's two

	mistakes out of two. A Saviour who is Christ the Lord has…
Trainee angel:	Died for us.
Sergeant angel:	Born. Been born for us. Where do they get these students from? Haven't you done any Jesus essays during the course?
Trainee angel:	Yes, I've done six GCSEs, six Jesus essays and all that coursework.
Sergeant angel:	Go on. What's the next bit? You will find him wrapped in…
Trainee angel:	You will find his clothes, but not him.
Sergeant angel:	I give up. Can you just try to get the last bit right? He has…
Trainee angel:	He has ascended, to be our Saviour.
Sergeant angel:	Descended. Has descended to be our Saviour. And you'll be descending too, if you don't watch out.
Gabriel:	*(coming on stage)* Having trouble, Sergeant?
Sergeant angel:	Sir! *(salutes)* Yes, sir. This young student here, she just doesn't know her nativity from her resurrection. She's got everything wrong.
Gabriel:	What did you say, trainee?
Trainee angel:	A Saviour who is Christ the Lord has died for us, in the city of Jerusalem. You will find his clothes, but not him. Christ is risen! He has ascended, still to be our Saviour.
Gabriel:	Well, that's perfectly correct.
Sergeant angel:	*(indignantly)* But not at Christmas, sir.
Gabriel:	It's always correct, especially at Christmas.

Christmas isn't just about a baby—it's the start of big amazing things. Jesus was born, so that he could teach us and save us and die for us. But you won't find him in a tomb because he rose again, to be our Saviour. He ascended into heaven, but he's still our friend and Saviour now he's there. Say it again, trainee.

Trainee angel: A Saviour who is Christ the Lord has died for us, in the city of Jerusalem. You will find his clothes, but not him. Christ is risen! He has ascended, still to be our Saviour.

Gabriel: That's the whole point of Christmas! I'm passing you to fly. *(Student flaps her wings and dances around.)*

Sergeant angel: I don't believe it! I don't know what heaven is coming to, sometimes, I really don't.

— Prayer —

For your own son as a baby born we thank you, Father God.
For your son risen in Jerusalem we thank you, Father God.
For a baby wrapped in newborn's clothes, we thank you, Father God.
For grave clothes folded in Jerusalem, we thank you, Father God.
For Jesus with us, Emmanuel, we thank you, Father God.
For Jesus, Saviour, Christ, our Lord, we thank you, Father God.

Developing the theme

This sketch could be used in school or uniformed groups with older primary-aged children. It may be helpful to set the scene for the children first. Ask what people have to do before they get their driving licence. Answers will include learning the controls, practising, and passing the theory and practical tests. Suggest that perhaps angels have to pass similar tests before they are allowed to become messengers for God.

* * *

St Paul's Day

Date: 25 January

Web link

www.ss-services.co.uk (for craft supplies to make bracelets)

Introduction

Paul is remembered for his dramatic conversion, his determined discipleship, his passion for mission and for the letters he wrote. The following idea for an activity session explores the main features of his life and work, and encourages people to think about their own faith and witness. It is also suitable as part of anniversary celebrations for churches that are dedicated to St Paul.

Key Bible verse

Then Saul, better known as Paul, was filled with the Holy Spirit.
ACTS 13:9

Bible links

- Mark 12:41–44 (a widow offers two coins)
- Acts 14:21 (Paul preaches the good news)
- Acts 16:16–40 (Paul in prison)
- Acts 24:24 (Paul speaks about having faith in Christ Jesus)

- Galatians 5:22–23 (the Holy Spirit produces good characteristics in us)
- Ephesians 6:10–18 (Paul advises people to put on all the armour that God gives)
- 2 Timothy 3:16 (everything in the scriptures is God's word)
- Philemon 1:19 (Paul writes with his own hand)

Key focus: Providing sacred space for reflection; sharing the Christian story

Key group: Church family; families; schools (particularly if they are dedicated to St Paul); uniformed groups

Activity ideas

Set up the meeting space with a different area for the activities associated with each of the six following focus words.

- Believer
- Traveller
- Prisoner
- Letter writer
- Preacher
- Teacher

Some of the activities will need tables and chairs. Each area should have its own leader to provide instructions and to guide the activity or discussion. After the gathering activity and the opening prayer, encourage everyone to visit each of the activities in whatever order they choose as there is no chronological element to the session. Suggest that families do the activities together.

Gathering

As everyone arrives, provide storybook versions of Paul's life to look at. Maps showing Paul's travels as a missionary may also be of interest. When you are ready to start, tell how Saul became Paul. Use sections 323, 324, 326 and 327 from *The Barnabas Children's Bible* (Barnabas for Children 2007, 2012) or similar material from a children's story Bible. Discuss what Saul (Paul) must have felt when Jesus spoke directly to him. Ask what his friends and family would have thought about the sudden change in him. Then pray before people move to the activity areas.

Prayer

Invite everyone to face in one direction. Pray for fun, good discussions and learning during the session as everyone discovers more about the life and faith of Paul. Then ask everyone to turn to face in the opposite direction to say 'Amen'.

Believer

Paul was a person of strong faith. He was passionate when he was persecuting the Christians, and he was even more passionate when he wanted to encourage people to believe in Jesus. Make bracelets to highlight the main things that Paul believed. Provide thin elastic and a range of beads. These can be bought from an educational supplier. Discuss what Paul believed and then invite people to select a different bead to represent each belief. His beliefs included the following.

- Jesus is Lord
- Jesus died for us
- Jesus defeated death after he was killed on the cross
- Jesus has opened the way for us to be friends with God
- Jesus brings us peace
- Jesus will return
- The Holy Spirit helps us to be gentle, kinder and more loving
- The value and power of prayer

- He, Paul, was called to preach to the Gentiles (people who were not Jewish)
- Scripture (the Bible) is the word of God

Once the bracelets have been made, invite people to decide which they think is the most important belief. Ask them to point to the bead that represents that on their bracelet.

Traveller

Provide a map of the Mediterranean area and then invite everyone to identify some of the places where Paul preached the good news about Jesus. Find the letters that Paul wrote in the index of a Bible and use their names to suggest the places Paul visited. Then use the maps in a study Bible to see where Paul travelled.

Alternatively, play a board game to explore Paul's travels together. The game can be found on page 196 and is also available to be downloaded from the website www.barnabasinchurches.org.uk/extra-resources/.

Prisoner

Act out the story of Paul and Silas in prison from Acts 16:16–40. Everyone can play the part of Paul if they wish. First ask everyone to make a short chain of paper links to shackle their feet together. Then huddle together, sitting on the floor. Sing a hymn of praise to God as Paul and Silas did. 'Our God is so great, so strong and so mighty' or 'Our God is a great big God' would be good choices. Then, as the earthquake comes, get everyone to rock from side to side before breaking out of their paper chains. Everyone stands up and, as the prison guard comes in to see what has happened, encourage them to shout: 'Have faith in the Lord Jesus and you will be saved!' (Acts 16:31). This could be repeated several times so that it is learned as a memory verse.

Letter writer

Paul wrote letters, or epistles, to encourage the early Christians in churches right round the Mediterranean. Provide postcards (along with pens and pencils) so that people can write or draw a picture to someone to encourage them in their faith.

Preacher

Paul preached about the good news of Jesus to hundreds of people in many different countries. Discuss where people can hear the good news about Jesus in your area. Church may be an obvious answer but also prompt thoughts about school, work, the internet and so on. Provide large plain biscuits, such as rich tea biscuits, and containers of water icing. Invite people to ice their biscuit and then decorate it with 'hundreds and thousands' of granulated sugar dyed with food colouring or chocolate sprinkles to represent all the people who will hear the good news of Jesus today.

Teacher

Paul used vivid imagery to teach people about faith. One of the most powerful is advising everyone to put on all the armour that God gives (Ephesians 6:11). Provide a set of play armour (belt, breastplate, shoes, shield, helmet and sword). This can be bought cheaply from a large toyshop or made beforehand. Ask a child to volunteer to be dressed up in the armour as Ephesians 6:10–18 is slowly read aloud. Talk about which bit of the armour—and what it represents in terms of faith—each person in the group most needs at the moment. Invite everyone to imagine putting on the piece of armour that they have just identified and then pray for the protection that God will provide through it for each person.

Saint

At the end of the session, gather everyone together. Remind them that Paul went from someone who persecuted Christians to someone who devoted his life to helping people believe in Jesus and to grow strong in their faith. Gather some ideas of 'one thing I want to remember from today' from the group. Challenge everyone during the coming week to find a way to remember something that Paul taught. Suitable hymns to sing, if required, include 'Be still, for the presence of the Lord' and 'Will you come and follow me if I but call your name?'.

— Prayer —

Jesus, you spoke directly to Saul to call him to faith. Help us to listen to you, and to learn from the life of the man who became Paul, the great apostle, so that we can grow in faith and share your good news with everyone.

Developing the theme

Use each of the six main aspects of Paul's life to plan further activities.

Believer

Ask older children to research how many Christian believers there are in the world at present. Invite them to create a PowerPoint presentation, or write something for the pew sheet or magazine, that gives information about where most of the world's Christians live. Provide a large map of the world and invite everyone to add a small sticker to indicate the different countries where they have Christian friends.

Traveller

Use the intercessions at a main service to pray for all who work in transport: bus, coach, lorry and train drivers; all who work to maintain transport systems and vehicles; everyone who works in aviation.

Prisoner

Contact the nearest prison to ask what support is needed to help the children of those visiting prisoners. There may be a need for new toys or for people to help with a crèche or play facilities.

Letter writer

Invite people to write a postcard of thanks to someone who has been a help or inspiration to them.

Preacher

Work together to choose one short Bible verse that the group would like to share with the world. Then ask everyone to post that verse on their Facebook or Moshi Monsters page, or Tweet it with a #hashtag so that it is possible to track how far the verse gets retweeted.

Teacher

Challenge everyone to share one of Jesus' stories with someone not at the event during the following week. A suitable story would be the poor widow who gave two coins for the temple offering (Luke 21:1–4). Share the story and then give each person two 2p coins as a reminder. Suggest that they use the coins when they tell the story and then give them to that next person so they have a reminder.

* * *

Granny and Grandpa Day

Date: 2 February

Introduction

2 February is also the day on which the feast of the presentation of Christ in the temple is celebrated. The Bible reading given in the lectionary for this day, and which many churches use on the nearest Sunday, talks of the amazing reaction that Simeon and Anna made when Mary and Joseph brought Jesus to the temple to be dedicated to God as required by the law.

Both Simeon and Anna are described as being of great age but they have an important part to play in the life story of Jesus. This makes an ideal occasion to celebrate the role that older people can play in the nurture of children in the church and give some of them an opportunity to talk about their faith.

Key Bible verse

Anna came in and praised God. She spoke about the child Jesus to everyone who hoped for Jerusalem to be set free.
LUKE 2:38

Bible links

- Leviticus 19:32 (respect older people)
- Psalm 148:12 (young and old will praise God)
- Zechariah 8:4–5 (young and old being together)
- Luke 2:22–35 (Simeon holds Jesus and praises God)

Key focus: Providing sacred space for reflection; sharing the Christian story

Key group: Children; church family; families

Activity ideas

If the children usually withdraw from the main service, arrange for some older people to visit the Sunday school or club to share some of the things they really value about following Jesus. This conversation could also take place in an all-age service or at a mid-week group.

Many children will be familiar from school with the idea of interviewing people, so make time for them to prepare some questions to ask their visitors. If they need prompting, good questions to explore might include the following.

- What was your favourite Bible story when you were a child?
- What is your favourite part of the Bible now?
- When did you first come to church?
- Who first brought you to church?

Be ready to ask a supplementary question, such as 'Why do you say that?' to help the discussion to move on from the merely factual and allow the older person to talk about their faith and the difference it makes in their life. For example, while it may be interesting to know that the person liked the account of the healing of Jairus' daughter, it is of more value to the children to know that it was because they identified with being the daughter or because they thought they would like to meet Jesus as the little girl did.

Prayer

Invite children to draw a prayer picture of a grandparent or an older member of their church that they want to pray for. Ask older people to draw a prayer picture of a grandchild or a young member of the church. They may want to write or draw a prayer request on the picture.

Developing the theme

Arrange for some older children to visit a residential home for older people to have the same discussion there. A small group of children could visit an older member of the church family who is confined to their home.

Mission ideas for Spring
(March, April and May)

*

St David's Day

Date: 1 March

Web link

www.celtnet.org.uk/recipes/cymraeg.php (for Welsh recipes)

Introduction

St David is the patron saint of Wales and 1 March marks his death in 589. He served as a bishop, and he went on pilgrimage to Jerusalem. The national celebrations of this day in Wales involve much singing, often followed by a *Te Bach* (tea with *teisen bach*— Welsh cake—and *bara brith*—Welsh fruit bread).

Key Bible verse

God Most High, I will rejoice; I will celebrate and sing because of you.

PSALM 9:2

Bible links

- Psalm 67:4 (nations celebrate with joyful songs)
- Jeremiah 31:13 (celebrate together)

Key focus: Building community relationships; fun

Key group: Local community; families

Activity ideas

Invite people to a traditional *Te Bach*. Decorate the meeting space with a Red Dragon flag, and display daffodils and leeks on the tables. Provide a 'pin the tail on the dragon' game and a trivia quiz of facts about Wales and St David. Arrange to learn one or two traditional Welsh songs such as 'Men of Harlech' as well as a hymn such as 'Guide me, O thou great Jehovah'. There may be someone who can help everyone to learn to sing one verse in Welsh. Older people will probably remember songs such as 'Men of Harlech', 'All Through the Night' and 'The Ash Grove' from school days.

Find the recipe for *bara brith* (translated as 'mottled bread'), a loaf made with dried fruit that has been soaked in tea, and *teisen*, so that you can provide authentic refreshments.

— Prayer —

For David and the saints of old, we give you thanks, O Lord.
For those who share God's word with us, we give you thanks, O Lord.
For songs to sing and food to share, we give you thanks, O Lord.
For special days and holy ways, we give you thanks, O Lord.

Developing the theme

Make contact with a church dedicated to St David. Try to find one in Wales if you are not based in the Principality, or elsewhere if you are in Wales. At the *Te Bach* write postcards of greeting to send to the partner church.

* * *

St Patrick's Day

Date: 17 March

Web link

www.bbc.co.uk/religion/religions/christianity/saints/patrick_1.shtml

Introduction

17 March is a day of celebration of St Patrick and Irish culture in general. Celebrations of the day, often based around a parade, are becoming more widespread across the United Kingdom. Patrick is remembered for his missionary work in Ireland and, allegedly, for using a shamrock—a three-leaved plant—to explain the doctrine of the Trinity.

Key Bible verse

Young women and young men, together with the elderly, will celebrate and dance, because I will comfort them and turn their sorrow into happiness.

JEREMIAH 31:13

Bible link

• Jeremiah 31:4 (dance and play the tambourine)

Key focus: Building community relationships; fun

Key group: Local community; families

Activity ideas

Invite everyone to wear something green (a traditional part of Irish celebrations) or offer the opportunity to make a hat or cap out of green crêpe paper. Provide green face-paint sticks so that everyone can have a shamrock drawn on to their cheek if they choose. Use green drapes to decorate the meeting space and, if using white paper cloths on the tables (or banqueting roll), provide green crayons or fibre pens so that everyone can draw shamrocks as decorations.

Another craft could be to make a tambourine from a paper plate, gluing strips of crêpe paper to dangle from the rim.

To create some Irish atmosphere, show part of a *Riverdance* DVD (see FAQs on page 13 for licence requirements for showing DVD clips). Challenge everyone to try to imitate the dancing. After some practice, parade around the meeting space. Those who prefer not to dance can mime the playing of instruments or line the 'route' and applaud the performers.

Share refreshments (something involving potatoes or soda bread would be an obvious choice).

— Prayer —

Part of the traditional hymn known as St Patrick's Breastplate makes a good prayer. Children will enjoy being led in simple movements to indicate where Christ can be found for each phrase.

Christ with me, Christ before me, Christ behind me,
Christ in me, Christ beneath me, Christ above me,
Christ on my right, Christ on my left,
Christ when I lie down, Christ when I sit down, Christ when I arise,
Christ in the heart of everyone who thinks of me,
Christ in the mouth of everyone who speaks of me,
Christ in every eye that sees me,
Christ in every ear that hears me.

TRANSLATED BY CECIL FRANCES ALEXANDER, 1889

Developing the theme

Discuss with a local residential home if they would like to host the St Patrick's Day celebration on their premises or if some of their residents would like to come and take part.

* * *

Stargazing

Date: end of March (before British Summer Time begins)

Web links

www.astronomyinyourhands.com
www.ras.org.uk/education-and-careers/educational-resources

Introduction

To respond to God with awe at the glory of his creation is a way in which Christians can worship God. Indeed, many people have come to faith because of the beauty and complexity of nature. Encouraging people to gaze in wonder at the stars is a way to share the astonishment described by the psalmist in Psalm 8.

Key Bible verse

I often think of the heavens your hands have made, and of the moon and stars you put in place.

PSALM 8:3

Bible links

- Genesis 1:16 (God made the stars)
- Nehemiah 9:6 (the people of Israel recognise that God made the stars)

- Psalm 8 (the wonders of the sky)
- Psalm 147:4 (God knows the stars by name)
- Isaiah 40:26 (God knows the number of the stars)

Key focus: Providing sacred space for reflection; fun

Key group: Church family; schools; local community; families; uniformed groups

Activity ideas

Find someone to lead a stargazing session. They do not have to be an expert as plenty of ideas and information can be downloaded from the websites noted above, but a local astronomical society may be able to offer an expert guide.

Start at the gathering point by inviting everyone to imagine how far away the stars are. They look tiny but we now know that they are huge compared to us. A couple of stars have been identified that are 100 to 200 times bigger than the sun, while some very old stars are somewhat smaller than the earth.

If the night sky is clear and without cloud it should be possible to identify the different stars that can be seen with the help of a night sky plan that can be downloaded from the internet. It may be necessary to move from the gathering point to somewhere that is shielded from light pollution so that better observations can be made.

If the weather does not allow stargazing, move indoors to look at the night sky plans. Share star-shaped biscuits, Milky Way® Magic Stars and hot chocolate, and plan another outing when the weather may be better.

Close the session by reading Psalm 8 and inviting everyone to reflect on the wonder of the universe.

— Prayer —

Spirit of God
Take our tiny imaginations
And open them to the whole
Reach of your astonishing creation.

Developing the theme

It may be possible to plan a trip to a local observatory if a small group becomes excited by the wonders of the night sky.

If someone in the church family is already proficient, or becomes so as the result of this activity, they could offer to help members of uniformed groups gain their astronomers' activity badge.

* * *

Earth Hour

Date: last Saturday in March

Web links

www.earthhour.org
www.wwf.org.uk

Introduction

Earth Hour is an annual, global event organised by the World Wide Fund for Nature that has been run since 2008. The aim is for everyone—families, businesses and institutions—to switch off their non-essential lights and appliances for one hour from 8.30pm local time to help everyone to focus on the link between use of resources and climate change. The mass switch-off of power that ensues gives a powerful message of concern.

Key Bible verse

I may be sitting in the dark but the Lord is my light.
MICAH 7:8B

Bible links

- Genesis 1:17–18 (God separates dark from light)
- Genesis 1:28 (God puts people in charge of the earth)
- Psalm 24:1 (The earth and everything on it belong to the Lord)
- Matthew 10:27 (What you hear in the dark, tell in the light)

Key focus: Campaigning and social action; fun; providing sacred space for reflection

Key group: Church family; families; local community; schools; uniformed groups

Activity ideas

Publicise Earth Hour as widely as possible through the local media and schools, and personal contacts of the church family. Provide a photo of someone switching off a light for the press.

Invite church families to use the hour of darkness to read a Bible story by candlelight. Light a single candle and thank God for the gift of light. Remind everyone that people have only been able to read the Bible by electric light for some 150 years. Keep a time of silence to relax into the near darkness. Use a standard Bible or a story version to read one of the following 'night-time' Bible passages.

- Genesis 15 (God's covenant with Abraham)
- 1 Samuel 3:1–10 (Samuel hears the Lord in the night)
- Daniel 6 (Daniel in a pit of lions)
- Matthew 25:1–13 (a story about ten girls)

- Matthew 26:36–75 (the night before Jesus died)
- Acts 20:7–12 (Paul preaches and Eutychus falls asleep)

Keep some silence at the end of the reading before inviting everyone to imagine themselves there in the dark at the time of the story. Discuss who the most important person in the passage is, what it might have felt like to be there, and whether it could happen today.

— Prayer —

Provide an individual tea light candle for each person present. Ask each of them in turn to suggest a situation or a place that needs God's light or a person who needs a particular blessing that night. As each person makes their request, light their candle from the original one. By the end, notice how much more light has been generated by these prayers.

Creator God, your light keeps shining in the dark, and darkness has never put it out. Help us to share your light and to protect the fragile resources of your world.

(BASED ON JOHN 1:5)

Developing the theme

Encourage families to have a regular 'Bible in the dark' time. Such activities create very special memories.

* * *

Easter story talk

Date: Holy Week or Good Friday

Introduction

For many schools Easter, like Christmas, is celebrated before the event. This idea for an all-age service on Good Friday, or for a school assembly, follows the journey Jesus made from coming into Jerusalem on a donkey through to his death and resurrection. Children present at a school assembly, which may take the form of an end-of-term service, or at a Good Friday service, may not come back to church for Easter Sunday. Therefore it is important to tell them the good news of the resurrection and to let them know that all becomes well.

Key Bible verse

'People of Jerusalem, don't be afraid! Your King is now coming, and he is riding on a donkey.'

JOHN 12:15

Bible links

- Matthew 21:1–11; 26:17–30, 36–56; 27:27–54; 28:1–9
- Mark 11:1–11; 14:12–26, 32–49; 15:6–38; 16:1–8
- Luke 19:28–38; 22:14–20, 39–53, 63–65; 23:26–47; 24:1–12
- John 12:12–19; 13:1–10; 18:1–12; 19:2–5, 16–29; 20:1–10

Key focus: Sharing the Christian story; providing sacred space for reflection

Key group: Church family; schools; children; families

Activity ideas

You will need a few large palm branches (real or made from paper);
a loaf of bread or a large roll; a towel; a toy sword; a purple cloak; a
standing cross; a plentiful supply of large heart-shaped confetti.

Make sure that there is a central aisle so that action can take place
in the middle of everyone.

Choose songs to illustrate the narrative as it proceeds (a selection
is included below). Be led in your choice of music by the songs
children already know, perhaps because they sing them at school. If
the session is taking place in a school assembly, avoid teaching a new
song if you visit the school only rarely (unless you are supremely
confident in your abilities). For the song 'Such love' point out that
each line starts with the words 'such love' and show the BSL signs
for 'truly' (meaning 'much' or 'true') and 'love'. Explain that each
verse ends with 'O Jesus' and again show the BSL signs. This then
becomes a very effective song with movement.

BSL signs

- **Truly:** Hold left hand out flat in front of body with palm facing
  upwards. Bring the right hand (held straight with palm facing to
  the left) down on to the left hand at right-angles as if you were
  trying to cut the left hand with the right.
- **Love:** Fold hands across heart.
- **O Jesus:** Point with right forefinger to left ring finger for 'O'.
  Then point with one forefinger to the palm of the other hand
  and then repeat using the opposite hands.

This website shows the signs being demonstrated (search for 'true',
'love' and 'o'):
www.signstation.org/index.php/bsl-dictionary/desktop-dictionary

Suggested songs

Near the beginning of the session

'Lord of the dance'
'We have a king who rides a donkey'
'For God so loved the world'
'When I think about the cross'

Just before the talk about Jesus' death

'Such love'

Near the end

'Easter Jubilation'

Talk

Leader: Imagine that you are in Jerusalem. Everyone is
talking about Jesus: the people he has healed, the
stories he has told, the miracles he has performed.
Some people are wondering if he really is the
king that the Jewish people have been expecting.
Suddenly a rumour goes round the crowd. Jesus is
coming and he is riding on a donkey. *(Point to the
back)* Yes, I can picture him coming in the distance.
And far away I can hear people chanting 'Ho-ho-
hosanna!'

*Go to the back of the meeting space and invite those sitting at the
back to join in the chant.*

*Gradually return to the front getting more and more people to
join in the chant so it gets louder and louder. After a while, signal*

for quiet and then ask if anyone is good at being naughty. Choose a volunteer and invite them to stand next to you.

Leader: People got so excited by the prospect of Jesus riding into Jerusalem that they did something a bit naughty. They pulled down branches from the palm trees. They started waving them in the air and throwing them on the ground in front of Jesus.

Give palm branches to the volunteer to wave. Then ask him or her to stand at the front holding their prop.

Leader: Then Jesus went to share a special meal with his friends, the disciples.

Ask if anyone likes cooking. Choose a volunteer and invite them to mime kneading some bread dough. Then hand them the bread to hold.

Leader: Jesus and his friends shared a meal that included bread and wine.

Ask the volunteer to stand at the front with their prop.

Leader: After they had eaten their supper, Jesus did something unusual.

Ask if anyone likes to have a bath. Choose a volunteer.

Leader: Jesus took a towel and washed his friends' feet.

Give a towel to the volunteer. Ask them to pretend to wash and dry the feet of someone sitting nearby, before joining the other prop-holders at the front.

Leader: Then Jesus took his friends to the Garden of Gethsemane to spend time in prayer. It was very quiet and the disciples fell asleep.

Ask who likes making a noise. Choose a volunteer and ask them to hold the toy sword.

Leader: While Jesus was praying, there was a terrible noise. Soldiers arrived to arrest Jesus.

Ask the volunteer to move around waving the sword and shouting, before joining the others at the front.

Leader: The soldiers took Jesus away. They mocked him.

Ask for a volunteer who likes dressing up.

Leader: The soldiers dressed Jesus in a purple robe and teased him saying, 'Are you really the king of the Jews?'

Put the purple robe on to the volunteer as he or she stands at the front.

Leader: It all becomes very sad now… but don't worry, the story does have a happy ending. Jesus was told he was going to be killed on a cross.

Stand a cross at the front of the meeting space with the volunteers behind it.

Leader: Jesus was nailed on the cross and he died. But because Jesus died, God opened the gates of heaven so that all his love could pour out on to our unhappy world.

Slowly tip a plentiful quantity of large heart-shaped confetti over the cross and pause.

Leader: And then, three days later, on the very first Easter Sunday, Jesus came back to life in a new way.

Prayer

The props from the Easter story invite us to pray if we wish. The palm branches invite us to praise Jesus for all the wonderful things he did. The bread reminds us to give thanks for the food we will eat today. The towel helps us remember that Jesus came to look after people and that he told us to look after other people too. The sword in this story is a symbol of violence so we may wish to pray for peace in the world. The purple robe reminds us that Jesus is now the king of heaven so we may want to worship him. Take a moment to choose which of these items will lead your prayer or reflection.

Next, invite everyone to keep silence together to bring their prayers to God. Allow at least 30 seconds for everyone to pray and then finish with the words, 'Lord Jesus, hear our prayers. Amen.'

Finally, invite everyone to come forward to take some of the heart confetti if they wish as a reminder of their prayers.

Developing the theme

This material will work in a children's group even if there is no space for movement. The artefacts can be used to provide a kinaesthetic dimension to the account.

* * *

Breakfast on the beach

Date: Anytime from Easter through to Ascension Day

Web link

www.magicbreakfast.com

Introduction

Many churches celebrate Easter or Ascension with an early service followed by breakfast. This idea encourages people to provide breakfast throughout the school year for hungry children in the UK through the Magic Breakfast charity.

Key Bible verse

Jesus said, 'Come and eat!'
JOHN 21:12

Bible link

• John 21:1–14 (Jesus eats breakfast with his disciples)

Key focus: Campaigning and social action; fund-raising for Magic Breakfast

Key group: Church family; local community; families

Activity ideas

At an Easter or Ascension Day breakfast, provide information about the Magic Breakfast organisation. £3.50 provides a nutritious breakfast for a child for a whole month. Invite people to make a donation if they have enjoyed the breakfast provided for them that morning. Alternatively, charge £2 per head for a simple breakfast and use the profit to make a donation.

— Prayer —

Lord of the morning, thank you that you invite your disciples to eat breakfast with you. Help us to be grateful for the wide choice of breakfast foods we have. Inspire us to be generous towards children who are hungry.

Developing the theme

£42 will provide breakfast for a child for a whole school year. Invite people to put coins into a jar every day on which they have breakfast to raise at least £42 by the end of the year. This is less than £1 a week, so it should be manageable for many families. Those living on their own could share a jar with a friend or two to raise money together—and they might choose to eat breakfast together once a month and to pray for the work of the charity. Some people may decide to choose a cheaper breakfast cereal occasionally to fund their donation.

A group of people could also organise a monthly cooked breakfast for the community. By making a reasonable charge, they could cover their costs and also use any profit to make a donation. People are more likely to attend a community breakfast if there is a fund-raising element.

* * *

St George's Day

Date: 23 April

Web link

www.scouts.org.uk

Introduction

St George is the patron saint of both England and The Scout Association. Some cub scout packs and scout troops will be glad of someone to visit their group to talk about St George. Schools may also welcome someone to talk about the patron saint of England.

Key Bible verse

Put on all the armour that God gives.
EPHESIANS 6:11

Bible link

• Ephesians 6:11–18 (the whole armour that God gives)

Key focus: Building community relationships; providing sacred space for reflection

Key group: Church family; schools; uniformed groups

Activity ideas

Explain that St George is traditionally thought to have been a

Roman soldier serving under the Emperor Diocletian. He is most unlikely to have killed a dragon, but George does seem to have been executed for being a Christian. Challenge cubs or scouts to work with their patrol to create a set of armour out of newspaper and sticky tape. Remind them to think particularly about protecting the head and chest, as well as creating a weapon with which to defend themselves. Allow about ten minutes for the activity so that everyone works at speed. By the end of the time each group should have one of their members arrayed in the armour. Ask each group to describe what they have produced and do some informal judging. This newspaper modelling could be used as a gathering activity before a service for St George's Day as it would take too long during the worship time.

Then introduce the concept of the 'armour' that God gives and read the passage from Ephesians. Discuss which bits of the armour listed would have been most useful for St George, and then which are the most relevant for scouts in the 21st century. Invite them to reflect on how they might remember to use this information each day as part of their preparation to keep their Scout Promise.

Prayer

Show a picture of a dragon and invite the scouts to think of a scary dragon in their own lives, such as bullying, poverty, unfairness and so on, that they would like to slay. Keep a time of silence and then invite everyone to sign 'Amen' by touching their fists together.

Developing the theme

If your church does not have close links with any or all of the uniformed groups in the area, use the opportunity provided by St George's Day to visit them. Take a basket of apples and wrapped Fairtrade cereal and chocolate bars as a goodwill gift.

* * *

Crib, cross, crown

**Date: Ascension Day; Christ the King Day (Sunday before Advent)
or any other time**

Introduction

Many children and families do not readily understand the sequence of the different phases of Jesus' life, from his birth through his ministry as an adult, to his death and resurrection, and to his ascension into heaven. This session encourages children to take part in activities that focus on three key aspects to discover Jesus as baby, man and king.

Key Bible verse

Keep your mind on Jesus Christ! He was from the family of David and was raised from death, just as my good news says.

2 TIMOTHY 2:8

Bible links

- Matthew 2:1–12 (Wise men visit Jesus)
- Luke 2:1–20 (Jesus is born and is visited by the shepherds)
- John 8:12 (Jesus is the light for the world)
- John 21:1–14 (Jesus eats breakfast with his disciples)
- Acts 2:22–36 (Jesus was crucified, raised from death and released the Holy Spirit)
- Revelation 1:9 (Jesus is our king)

Key focus: Sharing the Christian story; providing sacred space for reflection; fun

Key group: Children; church family; schools; families

Activity ideas

The suggested activities follow the sequence of Jesus' life. This means starting with Christmas activities that children will particularly enjoy outside December!

Visual display

Use a large table to display the majority of items that will be used during the session: candle; a bag for the story (see below); standing cross; heart-shaped confetti; purple fabric (to represent a royal robe); crown; apron; towel; bucket.

Gathering

Learn 'crib, cross, crown' hand signals to use during the session. For 'crib', cup hands together as if to cradle a tiny baby; for 'cross', make a cross sign with both index fingers; and for 'crown', use both hands to come down on to the head as a crown. Remind everyone to use the hand signals whenever they hear the phrase 'crib, cross, crown'.

Story

Use a light-hearted story version of the nativity story to remind everyone what happened. A good version is *The Story of the Star, the Stable and the Saviour* by Cameron Semmens (CWR, 2008).

Song

Sing 'The Virgin Mary had a baby boy', using actions. Children will not need words displayed to join in this song if you go through the words as you demonstrate the actions. Good actions for each verse are as follows.

The Virgin Mary had a baby boy (cradle arms to rock baby)
The angels sang when the baby was born (hands to mouth like a
  megaphone)
The shepherds ran when the baby was born (run on the spot)
The wise men travelled when the baby was born (Egyptian-style
  dancing, with one arm raised to be a camel's head and the
  other arm behind as the tail)

Craft

Crib biscuits

You will need three oblong-shaped biscuits, such as shortcake, per
person; squeezable tubes of ready-made icing; jelly babies; paper plates.

Place one biscuit on to the plate as the base, add a dab of icing in
the centre of the biscuit and press a jelly baby on to the icing. This
represents baby Jesus. Then squeeze icing along each short edge of
this biscuit and along one short edge of the second and of the third
biscuit. Use these two biscuits to assemble a 'roof' over the jelly
baby by forming a triangle with the base biscuit. More icing may be
needed to keep the structure firm.

Previously on 'crib, cross, crown'...

Summarise the story so far and remind everyone that Jesus was
born to be with us always, not just at Christmas.

Memory verse

Ask if any of the children have seen a Christingle. Ask them to
describe it (an orange, with a red ribbon wrapped around it,
decorated with four cocktail sticks loaded with sweets and fruit,
with a candle or glow stick in the top). Ask why it is important
to have the candle or glow stick on top of the orange. Once it has
been established that the candle represents Jesus as the light for the
world, help everyone to learn the following Bible verse.

Jesus said, 'I am the light for the world!' (John 8:12).

Light the candle on the display table and then repeat the memory verse again.

Story

Have a bag in which to keep the items for the story. The items can be produced one at a time, with explanation, to illustrate how Jesus was light for a dark world. If several of the children are familiar with stories about Jesus, invite the group to suggest why you have each item in your bag. Otherwise, explain why you have chosen the items—they all highlight aspects of Jesus' ministry during his life on earth.

- Tin of fish, such as tuna: to remind us that Jesus fed people with fish, or that Jesus called fishermen to be his followers
- Bandage: to remind us that Jesus healed people
- Water bottle: to remind us that Jesus turned water into wine, or that he said that he was 'living water'
- Boat: to remind us that Jesus used a boat as a platform to talk to people, or that he calmed the storm when the boat was caught up in it
- Heart: to remind us that Jesus cared for people
- Book of stories Jesus told: to remind us that Jesus was a wise storyteller
- Bread: to remind us that Jesus always gave thanks to God when he ate bread, including the time when he broke it at the Last Supper

Song

Sing 'Jesus' love is very wonderful' or something else known to the children that emphasises how much Jesus loves us.

Previously on 'crib, cross, crown'...

Remind everyone of some of the key points you have covered so far, emphasising the amazing and wonderful things that Jesus did for people. Then ask what happened next at the end of Jesus' life. What did people do to Jesus?

Standing cross and confetti

You will need a cross on a stand; heart-shaped table confetti.

Explain that Jesus was killed on the cross but that this meant that God's love could pour out of heaven on to us in a new way. As you speak, shake a plentiful amount of heart-shaped confetti over the cross so that it spills on to the table and, possibly, even on to the floor. Pause for everyone to reflect.

Response time

Offer a choice of decorating an individual small wooden cross (or one cut from card) with felt pens or of helping to arrange a large number of tea light candles into a cross-shape to be used in the closing reflection time later on.

Refreshment break

Take a break at this point.

Previously on 'crib, cross, crown'...

You will need purple fabric (to represent a royal robe); a paper crown; an apron; a towel; a bucket.

Ask if the cross was the end of the story of Jesus. No! Jesus came back to life in a new way. His friends saw him and shared breakfast with him. Then Jesus was taken up into heaven, where he remains as king! Ask if anyone knows why King Herod was so worried when

Jesus was born—because Herod was told that the new baby would be the king of the Jews. Invite one child out to be dressed as a king using the purple fabric and the crown.

Did Jesus behave like a king? No! What sort of things did he do? Invite another child out to be dressed in the apron, with the towel and bucket to hold. Remind everyone that Jesus washed his friends' feet.

Christians believe that Jesus is now the king of heaven. He was a baby in the crib (*do hand action*); he was a servant who died on the cross (*do hand action*); and now he wears a crown (*do hand action*) in heaven. And he is still our friend.

Reflection

Move so that everyone can gather around the cross-shape made out of tea light candles. Give a safety warning about keeping back from the candles. Then ask an adult to light slowly the candles as you invite everyone to think about what they have heard today. Keep a time of silence before using the prayer below.

Previously on 'crib, cross, crown'…

Quickly review the whole session by inviting everyone to make their own body sculpture for each of the words you use to highlight the material you have covered: baby, angel, sheep, star, camel, candle, light, fish, boat, heart, apron, bucket.

Game

Divide everyone into teams to play a relay race. Provide a set of objects for each team (tin of tuna, water bottle, towel, tea light). Each team has to pass one object at a time over the head of the first person and through the legs of the second person and so on until the object reaches the back of the line. The person at the end of the line then runs to the front and hands the object to their team supervisor before being given the second object to pass back in the same way. Play the game twice to ensure that everyone understands what they are doing.

— Prayer —

Stand in a circle and join hands. Then ask everyone to raise their hands to make a huge crown as you pray the following prayer.

Jesus, you were a king, but you were born as a baby and laid in a crib.
You lived as an ordinary person and helped people as a servant.
You died and came back to life in a new way.
Jesus, now you are our king in heaven but still our friend every day.
Thank you.

Developing the theme

This activity session could be offered at other times of the year such as straight after Christmas before children return to school, or following Easter.

* * *

Noah-by-numbers

Date: Sunday after Trinity Sunday

Web link

www.bgfl.org/bgfl/custom/resources_ftp/client_ftp/ks1/ict/ multiple_int/notes.htm (for information on learning styles)

Introduction

Noah is one of the better known passages in the Bible which appears in Year A of the Revised Common Lectionary. This is a fun way of providing a fresh presentation. It will also appeal to people who have a learning preference for numbers. Of course 'visual' learners would enjoy looking at a toy ark and 'kinaesthetic' learners will want to handle the ark and try to take it to bits as well as making the rain noise with their hands!

Key Bible verse

Be completely faithful to the Lord your God, love him, and do whatever he tells you.

DEUTERONOMY 30:20

Bible link

• Genesis 6:8—9:17 (the account of Noah)

Key focus: Sharing the Christian story

Key group: Children; church family; schools

Activity ideas

You will need eleven paper plates.

Put one numeral from 1 to 9 on separate plates, and 0 on the other two. Make these numerals as large as possible. Then put a small version of the appropriate number on the back of each plate to help with holding them up. Spread the plates out on a table so they are easy to pick up. Invite two people to help with holding up the numbers as they get mentioned. Children often enjoy seeing adults doing this not very well, but older children will manage it easily. Read out the story, emphasising the numbers and allowing time for those holding up the plates to find the correct one(s).

Leader: This is the story of (1) single man: Noah.

God had looked at the beautiful world he had made, and he was sad. Every (1) in the world was being nasty to every (1) else and they had forgotten about God.

Except (1) single man—yes, it was Noah! Noah was a good man who obeyed God.

God told Noah to build (1) big boat—we know it as Noah's ark. God told Noah to build it (130) metres long and (13) metres wide. Then God told Noah to load (2) of every kind of animal, bird and fish on to the boat.

And that is what Noah did. From aardvarks and antelopes, to meerkats and mussels, right through to the end of the alphabet: zanders, zebras and zebu. Then Noah got his (3) sons, and their wives, making (6), his own wife and himself aboard. All (8) of them.

And it started raining and raining...

Encourage everyone to make rain sound effects by tapping an index finger on to the palm of the other hand.

Leader: It rained for (40) days and (40) nights.

Every (1) on board the ark was safe—all (8) humans and (100s) of animals. But all the people and all the animals left outside were drowned.

After (40) days, it stopped raining but it was another (150) days before the water started to go down. Eventually it was safe for Noah and the (7) other people to get out of the ark, along with the (100s) of animals.

God was impressed with Noah, the (1) faithful person, so he made a covenant—a solemn promise—with Noah. God said, 'I will never destroy the whole earth again. As a sign of this promise I will create a rainbow of (7) beautiful colours.'

This is the story of (1) faithful man, whose name was Noah.

Craft

A craft idea to go with this story would be to use a bottle-style plastic milk carton. Before the session, lay the carton on its side (with the handle uppermost if it has one) and cut and remove the top surface. This creates a hollow shape that will float. Invite everyone either to paint the sides with brown acrylic paint mixed with some PVA glue, or to use PVA glue to stick craft lolly sticks on to the sides to represent the planks. Set aside to dry. Cut out some bookmark-style people (Noah and his wife) and animals from card and decorate. They will need to have a long stem so that they will appear above the side of the ark when placed inside. Use the ridged rim of half a paper plate to make a colourful rainbow. This can be glued to the outside of the ark or eased over the neck of the carton and held in place by screwing on the lid of the carton.

— Prayer —

O Lord, our God, you are the (1), the (1) and only. We worship you.
Jesus promised that where (2) or (3) are gathered in his name, he would be with us. So we praise you for being here with us now.
Thank you (4) the story of Noah, the (1) faithful man.
Help us to be faithful (2). When we (4)get, remind us with the (7) colours of your rainbow promise.

Developing the theme

Invite everyone to bring a cuddly toy to create a soft version of Noah's ark. Be ready to pair giraffes, elephants and dogs of widely differing sizes and styles. Use a very large cardboard packing case to create the ark into which all the cuddly toys will make their way.

Prayer rainbow

Create a rainbow prayer walk by using seven different rainbow-coloured A4 sheets plus two white ones. Write the prayer instructions for each colour on to the appropriate sheet. Spread out the nine coloured sheets of instructions with plenty of space in between them. Lead everyone through them, pausing at each station.

- **White**: stand quietly as you count up to ten in your head. Now hold your hands open as you tell God you are ready to chat.
- **Red**: think of seven amazing words to describe God. Then do one star jump as you call out each word to God (seven in total).
- **Orange**: stand on one leg as you thank God for all your favourite foods. Can you say them out loud as you balance?
- **Yellow**: mime lighting a candle. Pretend to hold it carefully as you thank God for sending Jesus to be the light for the world.
- **Green**: curl up in a ball like an animal sleeping. Thank God for summer and all the animals he has made.
- **Blue**: remember all the water in the story of Noah. Pretend to drink a cup of water as you ask God to help people who live in areas of drought.
- **Indigo**: sit quietly and remember something that has made you sad. Ask God to sort out the situation.
- **Violet**: look at your hand and remember three things that you have used it to do today. Ask God to help you use your hand to help him.
- **White**: finally, look back at all the colours and remember some of your prayers. Say or sign 'Amen'.

Mission ideas for Summer
(June, July and August)

*

Barnabas Bear

Date: 11 June

Introduction

The apostle Barnabas, whose name means 'One who Encourages', made many journeys, which we can read about in the Bible. Set up a 'Barnabas Bear pilgrimage' project in which a teddy bear (or other soft toy) takes the good news of the gospel from the church into the local community and beyond. Many infant schools have a similar project where a teddy journeys with different families so that young children can learn about travel and geography. Older church members may want to join in this project too.

Key Bible verses

They sent Barnabas to Antioch. When Barnabas got there and saw what God had been kind enough to do for them, he was very glad.
ACTS 11:22B–23A

Bible links

- Acts 4:36 (Barnabas was an encourager)
- Acts 9:27 (Barnabas was a helper)
- Acts 13:4 (Barnabas was sent by the Holy Spirit)

Key focus: Fun; providing sacred space for reflection

Key group: Church family; schools; local community; families

Activity ideas

Obtain a teddy bear (possibly from a charity shop) and select a name. Barnabas is a good name as it reminds us of Barnabas who accompanied Paul on his travels. However, you may wish to choose a name that links with the dedication of your church. Provide the bear with a small backpack, containing a notebook for families to note down prayer requests or answers, some memory verse cards, and the instructions for looking after the bear. It helps if you do the activity first and put your own comments into the notebook as an example.

The instructions might read: 'My name is Barnabas Bear. I like to help people to pray. I love to find out how families read the Bible, learn about God and how they try to live like Jesus or encourage each other in their faith. Please take a photo of me sharing prayer or reading the Bible or visiting a church while I am with you. Put a copy of the photo into my notebook and write something to explain what I am doing. Please bring me back to church next week (*or month*) so I can visit another family.' You may be able to establish a Facebook page to record the bear's adventures, too.

Introduce Barnabas Bear to the whole congregation when children are there. Briefly explain his purpose and then pray for his ministry and all the people who will help him. Pray for safe travelling, good relationships and fun family times.

Provide a calendar so that families can sign up for when they would like to look after the bear. Arrange a welcome back service for the bear at the end of the year so that the adventures can be celebrated by everyone. This could link with 'Bring your teddy to church' events at either end of the bear's adventures.

— Prayer —

Father God, please bless Barnabas Bear and everyone he meets on his travels. May this bear encourage lots of people to pray and to read the Bible. May Barnabas Bear make good friendships and enjoy times of family fun. Keep him safe on his journeys.

Developing the theme

This travel project for Barnabas Bear could also be developed as an RE project for an infant school, with the teddy being taken to visit the places of worship for different faiths.

* * *

Living streets

Date: early summer

Web links

www.livingstreets.org.uk
www.streetparty.org.uk

Introduction

Living Streets: Putting People First is a charity that campaigns for 'safe, attractive and enjoyable streets across the UK'. Their campaigns include proposing 20mph speed limits in residential streets, walk-to-school initiatives, encouraging everyone to walk more to improve health and reduce car use, and organising street parties (or street 'meets' if a full party is too much like hard work). The Street Party website has full instructions on applying for road closure or obtaining insurance, as well as plenty of ideas for activities.

Key Bible verse

Very old people with walking sticks will once again sit around in Jerusalem, while boys and girls play in the streets.

ZECHARIAH 8:4–5

Bible links

- Psalm 67:4 (nations celebrate with joyful songs)
- Matthew 5:13 (be like salt for everyone)
- Matthew 5:14–16 (be like light for the whole world)
- Luke 13:20–21 (God's kingdom is like yeast making the dough rise)

Key focus: Building community relationships; fun

Key group: Church family; families; local community; schools; uniformed groups

Activity ideas

Find an excuse to get everyone together! This could be a national event, such as a royal wedding or celebration, or something local like the tenth, 50th or 100th anniversary of a road or estate being built. Some parties can happen without a reason other than that a group of people think it is a great idea and are keen to work to make it happen.

If it is not possible to close a street, the church may be able to offer its drive or yard as a venue. Draw as many people as possible from outside the immediate church family into organising the event. A key aim is to strengthen friendships with other people, so avoid an approach that sees church members doing everything. Lots of the skills and resources needed for a good party will be out in the community. Organise a session beforehand to make bunting as this will get more people involved. It may be possible to invite a residential home, a nursery or a school class to make a single string to add to the display.

Plan some games or activities to keep children busy. If disposable banqueting roll is used to cover the tables, provide fibre pens or wax crayons to decorate the surface.

— Prayer —

As a church make a single string of bunting with joyful symbols or the 'fruits' of the Spirit listed in Galatians 5:22–23 (loving, happy, peaceful, patient, kind, good, faithful, gentle, self-controlled).

God of celebrations, show us how to reflect your light in our community; how to be salt to encourage the healing of relationships and yeast to build up the life we share.

Developing the theme

Look for another occasion to have a second party. A summer street event could be followed by a mini-party at 5pm on 31 December with everyone invited to light a tea light candle to represent their hopes and dreams for the New Year. At its simplest, provide a table and a supply of tea light candles with clean jars in which to place them—but the provision of hot chocolate or a mulled drink would encourage everyone to linger for a few minutes. Use an inexpensive gazebo that is quick to erect to provide a little shelter.

* * *

Open Farm Sunday

Date: mid-June

Web link

www.farmsunday.org

Introduction

Open Farm Sunday is an annual event to encourage people to meet the farmers who grow their food and care for the countryside. Farms that take part often offer guided tours, displays of farming machinery and a chance to meet the animals. The Bible reminds us that farming is a valuable occupation. For example, Noah farmed the land and planted a vineyard after the great flood. Jesus uses many farming examples in his parables.

Key Bible verse

'A few seeds make a small harvest, but a lot of seeds make a big harvest.'

2 CORINTHIANS 9:6

Bible links

- Genesis 9:20 (Noah the farmer)
- Psalm 65:9–12 (God brings about the harvest)
- Matthew 13:1–9 (the farmer who planted seeds)
- Matthew 13:24–30 (weeds growing among the wheat)
- James 5:7 (farmers wait patiently for rain)

Key focus: Building community relationships; fun

Key group: Church family; local community; families

Activity ideas

Offer practical assistance to any farm that is going to be open. They may need stewards to supervise car parking or to ensure that key gates are kept shut. They may want people to help serve refreshments or to oversee hand-washing facilities. Ask, and then be ready to help out. Otherwise, make sure to attend the event to support the farming community.

Urban and suburban churches could organise an expedition to visit an Open Farm.

— Prayer —

You take care of the earth and send rain to help the soil grow all kinds of crops. Your rivers never run dry, and you prepare the earth to produce much grain. You water all of its fields and level the lumpy ground. You send showers of rain to soften the soil and help the plants sprout. Wherever your footsteps touch the earth, a rich harvest is gathered. Desert pastures blossom, and mountains celebrate. Meadows are filled with sheep and goats; valleys overflow with grain and echo with joyful songs.
Creator God, we praise and thank you.

PSALM 65:9–12

Developing the theme

If relationships develop well, offer to hold a service of thanksgiving at the end of the Open Farm Day. Sing a well-known harvest hymn, give thanks for the work of the farmers and ask God to bless the land.

* * *

The Big Lunch

Date: June or July (join the national occasion)

Web link

www.thebiglunch.com

Introduction

The Big Lunch was started by the Eden Project in 2009 to encourage people to get together with their neighbours. In 2011 over a million people took part and in 2012 The Big Lunch was a key activity in the Queen's Diamond Jubilee celebrations.

Key Bible verse

How good and pleasant it is when God's people live together in unity!

PSALM 133:1 (NIV)

Bible links

* Genesis 18:1–8 (Abraham and Sarah provide a meal for angels)
* Isaiah 58:7 (share food with those who are hungry)
* Hebrews 13:2 (welcome strangers... they could be angels)

Key focus: Building community relationships; fun

Key group: Church family; schools; local community; families

Activity ideas

The easiest way to do this activity is to join in with an event that another community group is planning. Get involved to help their Big Lunch to happen. However, if there is no local lunch, take the lead. Try to avoid holding the event on church premises as this will mean that the community has to come to you. If at all possible, arrange to create the celebration in the playground of the local school or park or gather together people in a particular road to make it a street party. Work with the appropriate organisation (such as the school governing body or local authority) to gain permission. Draw as many local people as possible into the planning and organisation so that it does not remain a church event but a joint church and local community activity. The church may have equipment that can be loaned or helpers who have catering and food hygiene expertise.

Do not forget to include children and young people in the planning, organisation and delivery of the event. It is a great way to build relationships with a local uniformed group, for example.

There are plenty of ideas for everything from menus and recipes through to games and activities on the Big Lunch website, so you do not have to start planning from scratch.

— Prayer —

Father God, it is good when your people live together in unity. Thank you for this opportunity to get to know our neighbours and share a meal and fun with them. Help us to build real friendships through our Big Lunch.

Developing the theme

If the local community is already well organised for this event, consider hosting a special lunch for homeless people through the local hostel or soup kitchen. Another idea would be to provide a Big Lunch for children at a special school or members of a disability group.

* * *

Slow Food Week

Date: last week of June or at harvest time

Web link

www.slowfood.org.uk

Introduction

Slow Food is a global, grassroots, not-for-profit organisation that links the pleasure of food with a commitment to the community and the environment. It has members in more than 150 countries across the world. It aims to encourage people to think carefully about the food they eat and to encourage everyone to consider whether it is locally or sustainably produced rather than 'fast' and heavily marketed.

As Christians we recognise the sacred value of shared meals. This idea encourages churches to find ways of sharing in the preparation of a 'slow' meal.

Key Bible verse

Our God says, 'Calm down, and learn that I am God! All nations on earth will honour me.'
PSALM 46:10

Bible links

- Proverbs 12:27 (anyone too lazy to cook will starve)
- Micah 7:7 (wait for the Lord to answer prayer)

Key focus: Building community relationships; providing sacred space for reflection

Key group: Children, church family; families; local community; schools; uniformed groups

Activity ideas

Plan a half-day activity session that starts with the preparation of a simple but slow-cooked meal.

- Make bread from scratch.
- Make a simple soup so that a number of people, including children, can help with the washing, peeling and cutting up of the vegetables. This can be served in mugs, along with a spoon, if there are no bowls available. Avoid using disposable tableware as that does not fit with the 'slow food' approach. Sharing in the washing-up afterwards will be all part of the experience.
- Provide a selection of cheeses so that everyone can taste a range and talk about the different flavours.

Once the food is slowly cooking, this may be the moment for a coffee or tea break. Then set about creating an attractive space for everyone to eat together. Encourage people to help lay the tables. Invite everyone to make a placemat for someone else using fibre pens on a sheet of A4 paper. Check that enough placemats have been made to provide one for each person, and ask for a few more to be made if necessary. A small all-age group could create mini flower arrangements in little glass jars using either wild flowers gathered outside or simple blooms from a garden or market stall. Another group could create place names for everyone. A third group could write a grace to say at the beginning of the meal.

With the tables laid and the food under way, now is the time to share some simple games. Play Kim's game (p. 190), using 20 food and meal items on the tray, for example, an apple, carrot, fork, jar of jam, (safe) knife, onion, pepper mill, potato, napkin, spoon, tin of tuna, teabag, tin opener, egg cup and so on.

In groups of three to six people play a pizza variation of 'Beetle'. Players have to throw 6 to start so they can draw the pizza base. The subsequent numbers can be drawn in any order: 5 to add a tomato layer, 4 to add a cheese topping, 3 to add a mushroom and 2 to add a pepperoni slice (both of these can be added more than once), and 1 to add a sprinkle of herbs. The winner is the first to complete their pizza by throwing all numbers from 1 to 6.

Prayer

Help us to slow down, Lord, and to get to know each other. Help us to relax as we enjoy our slow-cooked food together. Help us to be still and know that you are God.

Developing the theme

Many families do not have the time or skills to make 'slow' meals. Arrange some after-school sessions for families to prepare a simple meal and share new recipes together. Either cook and eat the meal there and then, or encourage people to make and assemble the food, and then take it home to finish so they can eat with all the family. In some areas local health authorities may be able to assist with funding such a project.

✻ ✻ ✻

Get wet party

Date: in the summer months

Web link

www.tapwater.org

Introduction

Tapwater.org is a not-for-profit organisation that promotes the drinking of tap water in the UK. Their aim is to reduce the quantity of expensive and environmentally-damaging bottles of water consumed annually by making it easy to get access to tap water when people are out and about. This idea is for a 'get wet' party to highlight the delights of tap water for games and for drinking.

Key Bible verse

On the last and most important day of the festival, Jesus stood up and shouted, 'If you are thirsty, come to me and drink!'
JOHN 7:37

Bible links

- Psalm 107:9 (God gives drink to thirsty people)
- Proverbs 25:25 (cold water refreshes thirsty people)
- Hosea 13:5 (God cares for people in a thirsty desert)
- John 4:13 (everyone who drinks water will be thirsty again)
- Revelation 21:6 (water for everyone from the life-giving fountain)
- Revelation 22:17 (life-giving water is free)

Key focus: Campaigning and social action; fun

Key group: Children; church family; families; local community; schools; uniformed groups

Activity ideas

Organise a 'get wet' party that will last for an hour. This could be in someone's garden, providing a risk assessment is made, or in a public park with permission from the appropriate authority. If you use a public space, make it an all-age event with parents and carers expected to stay as it is difficult to create an enclosed space for children left in your care. You will need a plentiful supply of water. The advantage of this idea is that it will not matter if it rains. Rain will not stop play as getting wet is the point of the event! Invite everyone to come in swimming costumes, covered with old T-shirts and shorts, and wearing plimsolls or training shoes. Explain that flip flops or bare feet will not be safe for the activities provided.

Gathering activity

Play skittles using used water bottles half-filled with water. Provide several sets so a number of children can play at once. If there is a paved area available, provide water pistols or washing-up liquid bottles filled with water and invite children to draw a masterpiece in water.

Water games

Cup of water relay

Divide into teams and for each team provide a bucket of water at the start line and an empty bucket at the finish. Team members stand in a line between the start and the finish. At the word 'go', the first person in each team has to fill a plastic beaker with water from the bucket and pass it to the next person in the line. The team passes the beaker along the line until the last person empties it into the second bucket. They then run back to the beginning to start the process again. Play the game with a single beaker per team for about two minutes and find the winning team according to the most water transferred. Then replay the game but provide six beakers per team so that the whole activity becomes much more exciting, hectic and wet! A third variation is to provide plastic beakers that have a few small holes punched in them so that the water drains out as they are passed along.

Sponge relay

This game is played in the same way as the cup of water relay, but by transporting the water in a large car washing sponge. Play this towards the end of the event as everyone will get very wet.

Ice cube and spoon

This is a variation on 'egg and spoon'. Either play it as a relay, or give everyone an ice cube and a dessert spoon in which to carry the ice cube down the race track.

Musical washing-up bottles

Ask everyone to sit in a circle. Fill a clean and empty washing-up liquid bottle with water. The bottle is passed round while the music plays. When the music stops, the person holding the bottle has to give two squirts of water each to the person on their left and on their right. If the circle is large, provide more than one bottle of water.

Puddle jump

Provide a long skipping rope turned by two teenagers or adults. Give everyone a full plastic or paper cup of water to hold and then challenge them to dart into the turning rope, jump over it six times as it turns and then run out. With a large group of people, provide more than one rope.

Water balloon toss

Fill balloons with water and make sure you have some spare. Organise everyone into teams of equal number. Play a relay race with the balloons being thrown from player to player down the team line with everyone standing a few feet apart. If a balloon bursts, that team has to start again with a new balloon.

Water limbo

If you can organise a working hose, challenge everyone to limbo dance under a stream of water.

Water pistol tag

Choose someone to be 'it' and give them a loaded water pistol with which they have to try to 'tag' the players as they run round. Once a player has been caught by a jet of water, he or she must stand still until another player frees them. This would also work with 'it' using a large wet sponge to tag the players.

Refreshments and talk

Provide tap water for everyone to drink (if desired, added to fruit juice or a squash). Chunks of watermelon will also be welcome if the weather is hot. While refreshments are being served, talk about the huge amount of bottled water (over two billion litres) consumed in the UK each year. Millions of plastic water bottles end up in landfill every day. Christians remember that Jesus described himself as 'living water'.

At the end of the party give everyone information about tapwater. org so they can find out more about this organisation and join the campaign if they wish.

— Prayer —

Generous God, thank you for the streams of life-giving water you give us in Jesus. Thank you for the streams of thirst-quenching water we can get from our taps. Thank you for the technology and hard work of people to provide this water. Help us to be wise about the water we drink and buy. Please help us to look after the wonderful world you created by not using too many plastic bottles.

Developing the theme

Some churches, schools and uniformed groups may choose to campaign to reduce the number of bottles of water they buy collectively. Apart from encouraging their own members not to buy bottled water, they could also try to encourage shops and other places to become refilling stations. Another idea would be to do some fund-raising to fund a mains-fed water machine in a school or buy a set of tapwater.org bottles for members.

* * *

Summer fête

Date: during the summer

Introduction

It is valuable for a church to be seen 'at play' and taking part in community activities. This is a simple idea that will take little preparation and comparatively little kit. The value of the activity is that it will provide many opportunities to chat, particularly with family members, as others play skittles.

Key Bible verse

Always be joyful and never stop praying.
1 THESSALONIANS 5:16–17

Bible link

• 1 Timothy 2:8 (let everyone pray)

Key focus: Building community relationships; fun; providing sacred space for reflection

Key group: Church family; schools; local community; families

Activity ideas

Take a stall or stand at a summer fête or village show. Create a miniature skittle alley (if you have access to traditional wooden skittles, you could use those too). If the stall is to be on grass, consider using a folding table, without the legs extended, as a smooth base. Use the cardboard inner tubes from catering-size disposable paper roll (domestic tubes are likely to be too flimsy). Put a different prayer topic as a label on each of the nine skittles as follows and provide some soft balls.

- Amazing God
- Praise
- Pray for a person
- Pray for a country
- Pray for yourself
- Question
- Silence
- Sorry
- Thank you

Invite passers-by to play prayer skittles. Explain that it is free and all that is required is to roll (or toss) up to three balls to knock down one or more skittles. If the player scores a hit, discuss who or what they would like to pray for relating to the category marked on the skittle they have knocked down. Children will be particularly good at coming up with suggestions. Provide pens, note paper and a large box so that people can record and post their prayers if they wish. All the prayers can then be offered again to God at the end of the event.

Give everyone who takes part a sticker with the words, 'I have played prayer skittles' or 'I have prayed and played'. The stickers can be printed via a computer and have the image of a skittle alongside the wording.

— Prayer —

God of fun, thank you that you make it easy to take the first steps in prayer. Guide us to listen carefully to the prayer requests that people make, and their conversations, and to respond sympathetically. We offer you all the prayers that will be made today and we pray for the people who will make them.

Developing the theme

Prayer skittles are a fun activity in any all-age or children's group. Provide plain skittles and invite people to come up with ideas to put on the labels.

* * *

St Mary's Day

Date: 15 August, or other dates associated with Mary such as 25 March (the Annunciation)

Web links

www.jesusmafa.com
Search online for 'Turvey Abbey pictures of Jesus and Mary'

Introduction

This is an idea for an activity session that looks at the whole life of Mary, the mother of Jesus, in a chronological way. It could be run in a children's group or for all ages together. The idea would work well to celebrate the patronal festival of a church.

Key Bible verse

Mary kept thinking about all this and wondering what it meant.
LUKE 2:19

Bible links

- Matthew 1:18–24 (Joseph and Mary)
- Matthew 2:1–12 (the visit of the wise men to Jesus)
- Matthew 2:13–14 (Joseph takes Mary and Jesus into Egypt for safety)
- Matthew 27:56 (Mary was watching as Jesus died)
- Luke 24:1–8 (women bring spices for Jesus' body)
- Luke 1:26–38 (Angel Gabriel tells Mary she is to have a special baby)
- Luke 1:39–56 (Mary visits her cousin, Elizabeth, and praises God)
- Luke 2:1–7 (Mary and Joseph travel to Bethlehem and Jesus is born)
- Luke 2:8–20 (the visit of the shepherds)
- Luke 2:22–38 (Mary and Joseph present Jesus to the Lord in the temple)
- Luke 2:39–40 (Mary and Joseph take Jesus home to Nazareth)
- Luke 2:41–52 (Jesus talks to the Jewish leaders in the temple)
- John 2:1–11 (Mary tells Jesus to provide wine at a wedding)
- John 19:25–27 (Jesus tells John to look after Mary)
- Acts 1:14 (Mary was with the apostles when they met to pray)

Key focus: Providing sacred space for reflection; sharing the Christian story

Key group: Children; church family; families; local community; schools (particularly if they are named St Mary's)

Activity ideas

You will need one person to act as a narrator and explainer of activities, and the following words written large to form the timeline of Mary's life.

- Listening
- Visiting
- Praising
- Travelling
- Wondering
- Presenting
- Escaping
- Searching
- Directing
- Watching
- Mourning
- Praying
- Continuing

The suggested activities follow the sequence of Mary's life. Choose as many as are practicable for the time and space available but try to ensure that the whole of Mary's life can be considered.

Create a quiet, reflective space in one corner of the room with comfortable chairs or beanbags. Display some artefacts to illustrate aspects of Mary's life such as an angel, a map of the Bible lands including Egypt, a crib, a wine bottle and a standing cross.

Download some different images of Mary (see web links above). Provide some storybooks that tell aspects of Mary's life and copies of the Bible with references to Mary clearly marked.

Gathering

Names are an important part of Mary's story. Invite everyone to make a name badge or sticker to wear as everyone is arriving.

Set the scene

Explain that today you are going to think about Mary, the mother of Jesus: who she was, what she did and how she can inspire us. Ask what people already know about Mary. Take some answers before moving to the next activity.

Listening

Talk about how Mary was someone who really listened to God. Introduce the story about what happened when the angel Gabriel visited Mary with a message. Read Luke 1:26–38 from a children's Bible.

Discussion

In small groups of three or four people, discuss the following questions. Younger children will need an older child or adult to help them answer the questions.

- Why do you think God chose Mary to be the mother of Jesus?
- What would have happened if Mary had said 'no'?

Visiting

Talk about the time that Mary set off to visit her cousin, Elizabeth. Point out that she was given a very warm welcome. Invite everyone to find at least two people they do not know very well and say 'hello' to them. This could be the appropriate time to offer some refreshments, although it may be better to wait until everyone is busy making their spice jar.

Praising

Explain that after Elizabeth greeted her so warmly and confirmed that she knew about the special baby she was bearing, Mary began praising God extravagantly. Sing a favourite song to praise God and encourage everyone to dance. Alternatively, invite everyone to suggest phrases to describe how amazing God is and record them on to a large sheet of paper using bright colours. This can then be displayed on a wall.

Travelling

To help everyone to understand how much travelling Mary had to endure when she was pregnant, play a game of 'Follow my leader'.

Leader: Mary had to walk back from Elizabeth's home…

All mime walking slowly.

Leader: Mary set off, with Joseph, from Nazareth to
              Bethlehem…

All mime walking. NB: as there is no mention of a donkey in the story, do not mime riding on a donkey.

Leader: Mary and Joseph tried to find somewhere to stay…

All mime knocking on doors.

Leader: But there was no room for them…

All mime shaking heads.

Leader: And they had to keep on walking...

All mime walking.

Leader: Eventually they found some space in a shelter by an inn...

All mime finding shelter by pointing.

Leader: Mary was exhausted as she gave birth to her first son...

All mime cradling a baby.

Wondering

Divide into groups of up to ten people. Provide each group with a crib set (packed into a box or basket), a candle (unlit) and a base cloth. Sit around in a circle. Spread the base cloth in the centre and then slowly unpack the crib figures and arrange them. When all the groups have done this, arrange for the candle in each group to be lit by an adult. Remind everyone that Mary was young. She had been approached by an angel and told she would have a very special baby. Now she and Joseph and Jesus had been visited by shepherds and some wise men. What did she do? The Bible tells us that Mary kept thinking about all this and wondering what it meant (Luke 2:19). Invite everyone to sit and wonder in silence for a few moments—just like Mary. (Allow at least a minute so that everyone can settle down into the silence.)

Presenting

Talk about how Mary and Joseph presented Jesus to God in the temple (rather as we might dedicate or have a service of thanksgiving for the gift of a new baby). Use the baby Jesus figure from one of the crib sets to pass around the group, taking great care not to drop it. As each person holds the figure, invite them to say out loud, 'Thank you, God, for sending us your son, Jesus.'

Escaping

Explain that after the visit by the wise men, Joseph was warned by an angel in a dream to take Jesus and Mary to Egypt to keep them safe from Herod. Play 'What's the time, King Herod?' to represent the Holy Family escaping from Herod. This game is a version of 'What's the time, Mr Wolf?' (p. 193).

Searching

Explain that Mary and Joseph used to take Jesus to the temple each year for the Passover Festival. One year, when he was twelve years old, they realised that Jesus was not with them as they travelled back to Nazareth. They had to return to Jerusalem to search for him.

Play a game of 'Hunt Jesus in the temple' by hiding a small picture of Jesus somewhere in the meeting space and encouraging everyone to search for it. Re-hide the picture after it has been found so that several people can find the picture. This game is a version of 'Hunt the thimble' (p. 190).

Directing

Read the account of Jesus turning water into wine from a children's Bible. Use the name 'Mary' rather than the phrase 'Jesus' mother'. Get everyone to practise movements for key words in the text.

- Mary (cradle a baby)
- Jesus (use each index finger in turn to point to the palm of the opposite hand)
- Wine (drink from a goblet)
- Water (pour water from a jug)
- Servants (bow head)

Discuss whether Jesus was pleased that Mary told him what to do. Why did Mary ask Jesus to get involved?

Watching

The Bible tells us that Mary was standing close to the cross when Jesus was crucified (John 19:25). Provide a large sand-filled egg timer and ask everyone to stand and watch with Mary as the sand trickles through. Alternatively, play a game of 'Sleeping lions' (p. 192), only with everyone having to keep their eyes open.

Mourning

Tell how women, who probably included Mary, brought spices to anoint Jesus' body. Provide ingredients to make some potpourri.

You will need cinnamon sticks broken into pieces; whole cloves; whole allspice; whole peppercorns and, if available, pieces of dried orange peel and dried rose petals; empty and clean baby food jars; gauze, net or muslin cut into circles; ribbons or small rubber bands for each jar.

Use teaspoons to add a little of each ingredient to a small baby food jar or mini jam jar. Leave a little gap at the top of the jar. Seal the jar with a circle of gauze, net or muslin, tied on with string or ribbon or fastened with a small rubber band. When shaken, the spices will release their perfume.

Praying

Mary met frequently with the apostles to pray after Jesus had risen to heaven. Divide into the same groups used for the wondering activity above. Relight the candle for each group and talk about what everyone has learned about Mary during the session. Then invite each person to pray about what they hope to remember or what they want to thank God for from the session.

Another way to do this would be to provide a picture or symbol for each of the activities completed as follows.

- Listening (a Bible)
- Visiting (the word 'hello')
- Praising (some bright fabric)
- Travelling (a map)
- Wondering (the lit candle)
- Presenting (the baby Jesus figure from the crib set)
- Escaping (a footstep cut from paper)
- Searching (the number twelve written as a numeral)
- Directing (a water bottle)
- Watching (a small cross)
- Mourning (the spice jar)

Continuing

Gather everyone together to issue the continuing challenge. Explain that Mary's story has not come to an end. We have been able to learn more about God the Father and Jesus today because of Mary. What can each of us do to share the good news of Jesus with people we meet this week? Take some time to gather suggestions.

Prayer

Marigolds were traditionally supposed to have been named 'Mary's Gold' in honour of Jesus' mother. There is a legend that Mary used the flowers from marigolds as coins and, on the flight into Egypt, thieves stole her purse and marigold flowers fell out.

When beginning to pray about this session, and to make plans, plant marigold seeds in individual pots. Give a pot to each person who will be involved in making the event happen, as a reminder to pray as the plant develops. It may be possible to grow plenty of marigolds so that each family can take one home from the session.

Developing the theme

With permissions from the parents/carers, take photographs of the different activities as they happen. These can be printed to provide a pictorial celebration of the life of Mary—a helpful illustration of her importance, particularly for a church dedicated to St Mary.

Mission ideas
for any time

*

Alternative birthday present challenge

Date: anytime

Web links

www.actorsbenevolentfund.co.uk
www.c-r-y.org.uk
www.freecycle.org
www.lifesavers.org.uk
www.powerinternational.org
www.slsgb.org.uk
www.trusselltrust.org/foodbank-projects
www.throughtheroof.org
www.twam.co.uk

Introduction

While most enjoy receiving birthday presents, many people are starting to question whether they wish to be given more goods or even experiences at Christmas or for their birthday. This has been proved by the popularity of 'alternative' presents, whereby people are told a goat, water well or similar has been given to a community or area in need in honour of their special occasion. Most alternative presents are offered by the larger charities, as smaller organisations cannot provide this option. The idea of an alternative birthday present challenge will encourage people to seek out a wider range of charities to support.

Key Bible verse

Each of you must make up your own mind about how much to give. But don't feel sorry that you must give and don't feel that you are forced to give. God loves people who love to give.

2 CORINTHIANS 9:7

Bible links

- Acts 20:35 (blessings come from giving)
- 2 Corinthians 9:12 (your giving may prompt others to give thanks to God)
- Hebrews 13:16 (remember to help others and to share your possessions)

Key focus: Fun; fund-raising for charity

Key group: Church family; schools; local community; families

Activity ideas

The birthday person tells their family and friends that they would prefer not to receive actual presents. They would welcome money in lieu to be given to a charity of the donor's choice. The challenge—and the fun—is for the giver to donate their money to a charity that is appropriate to the birthday person. The giver then tells the birthday person the name of the charity and the reason why they chose it for them. Examples of different interests and appropriate charities include:

- Computer geeks: Tools with a Mission (refurbished computers to Africa)
- Dog owners: Guide Dogs for the Blind
- Gardeners: Practical Action (provide seeds)

- Motor racing fans: Action for Kids (provides motorised wheelchairs)
- Theatre goers: Actors' Benevolent Fund
- Keen swimmers: Surf Life Saving GB

Other ideas include:

- Cardiac Risk in the Young (for someone who has a big heart for life)
- Freecycle UK (for the world's greatest re-cycler)
- Power International (thanks for being a strong person in my life)
- Royal Life Saving Society (for someone not known for their DIY skills)
- Through the Roof (have a great party that raises the roof!)

— Prayer —

Generous God, you have created us in your image to be generous too.
Help us to include those less fortunate in our times of celebration.
Inspire us to be inventive as we search for charities to support
in this challenge.

Developing the theme

A whole family might choose to receive just one small present each for Christmas, with everyone working together to search for an appropriate charity to reflect the interests of each family member.

* * *

Crazy Bible hats

Date: anytime

Web links

www.biblegateway.com
www.crazyhatsbreastcancerappeal.co.uk

Introduction

Crazy Hats is a charity based in Northamptonshire. It raises money to support people undergoing treatment for breast cancer by organising events at which people wear 'crazy' hats (often pink). Their vision and enthusiasm encouraged me to develop this idea to challenge people of all ages to create a hat to represent a character in the Bible, while raising funds for charity.

Key Bible verse

Kindness and justice were my coat and hat.

JOB 29:14

Bible link

- Proverbs 1:8–9 (wear your parents' teaching like a lovely hat)

Key focus: Fun; fund-raising for charity; building community relationships; sharing the Christian story

Key group: Children; church family; families; local community; schools; uniformed groups

Activity ideas

Organise a crazy hat festival in which people have to make and wear a hat that represents a character in the Bible. Start by asking a couple of families to make their creations in advance so that they can be photographed. Use these photographs in press releases as all newspapers like an unusual picture. Also set up a Facebook page where the photographs can be posted and where participants can start to share ideas about which Bible person they will choose (and why) and what materials they are thinking of using.

Ask people for donations to enter the competition and make a small charge for refreshments at the actual event.

In the publicity give some suggestions with brief details of the character, plus a Bible reference as a prompt to look the characters up. Include a Bible website, such as www.biblegateway.com, to enable people to access scripture even if they do not have a Bible at home. Make it clear that other Bible characters not on the list can be chosen too.

Suggested characters

- Adam: the first man, asked to name the animals (Genesis 2:7–20)
- Eve: the first woman, liked fruit (Genesis 3:1–13)
- Noah: builder of the ark (Genesis 6:9–22)
- Abraham: entertained angels (Genesis 18:1–8)
- Lot's wife: looked back and was turned to a block of salt (Genesis 19:26)
- Joseph: had an amazing coat (Genesis 37:3–4)
- Moses: saw ten plagues come to Egypt (Exodus 7:14—11:9)
- Joshua: won the battle of Jericho (Joshua 6:7–20)
- Ruth: worked in Boaz's field (Ruth 2)
- David: shepherd, musician and king (1 Samuel 16:19; Psalm 108:1; 2 Samuel 2:10)
- Solomon: was very wise (1 Kings 3:9)

- Daniel: spent a night with the lions (Daniel 6)
- Esther: a beautiful queen (Esther 2:7–8, 17)
- Job: suffered terrible troubles, but didn't lose his faith in God (Job 19:25–27)
- Isaiah: a prophet who foresaw the birth of Jesus (Isaiah 9:6–7)
- Gabriel: an angel and messenger from God (Luke 1:26–38)
- Mary: mother of Jesus (Luke 2:1–7)
- Shepherd: hurried to see baby Jesus (Luke 2:16)
- Wise man: brought a gift to Jesus (Matthew 2:11)
- Herod: wanted to have baby Jesus killed (Matthew 2:13, 16)
- Jesus: God's only son; baby, boy, teacher, healer, friend, king (John 3:16)
- John the Baptist: prepared the way for Jesus (Mark 1:1–4, 7–8)
- Peter: fisherman and disciple (John 1:40–42)
- Matthew: tax collector turned disciple (Matthew 9:9)
- Zacchaeus: climbed a tree to see Jesus better (Luke 19:1–9)
- Jairus' daughter: was healed by Jesus (Mark 5:21–24, 35–43)
- Martha: friend of Jesus who busied herself with housework (Luke 10:38–42)
- Mary, sister of Martha: poured perfume over Jesus' feet (John 12:3)
- Pontius Pilate: washed his hands as a sign that he didn't want to be involved (Matthew 27:24)
- Barnabas: encouraged people (Acts 4:36–37)
- Paul: escaped from Damascus in a basket, prisoner, letter-writer (Acts 9:25; 16:37; Colossians 4:18)
- Lydia: sold expensive purple cloth (Acts 16:14)
- Damaris: put her faith in God (Acts 17:34)
- Eutychus: went to sleep and fell out of a window (Acts 20:9–10)
- Nympha: hosted a church in her home (Colossians 4:15)

Organise a coffee morning or a tea party at which people are invited to wear their hats for the grand judging. Offer prizes for the largest hat and the most inventive materials, as well as for different age groups and the 'best in show'. Make sure that the judge comes from outside the area! Provide some hat-designing pages for children to colour in as an activity at the event. It may be possible to interview some of the entrants about why they chose their Bible character.

If it is possible to organise a parade of hat-wearers, try to get everyone to line up in the order in which the characters appear in the Bible. It does not matter if several people have chosen the same character as the hats will all be different. Take a group photograph as well as pictures of the individual winners to issue to the press and to post on Facebook.

— Prayer —

Hats to protect and hats to adorn
Hats to raise money and hats to be worn
Hats to prompt smiles and hats to impress
We ask you, Lord Jesus, our efforts to bless.

Developing the theme

Arrange some hat-making sessions to build community relations. Offer to take the activity to residential homes. Provide materials from a local scrap store to save having to buy too many.

* * *

Micah challenge

Date: anytime

Web links

www.embracethemiddleeast.org
www.compassionuk.org
www.micahchallenge.org.uk
www.wvi.org

Introduction

Micah Challenge is a global movement encouraging Christians to be committed to the needs of those who live in poverty. The charity campaigns to halve poverty by 2015 with a focus on the eight Millennium Development Goals (MDGs) as follows.

- End poverty and hunger
- Achieve universal primary education
- Promote gender equality and empower women
- Reduce child mortality
- Improve maternal health
- Combat HIV/Aids, malaria and other diseases
- Ensure environmental sustainability
- Develop a global partnership

The Christians who lead the Micah Challenge see their campaign as the practical outworking of the following Bible verse.

Key Bible verse

The Lord God has told us what is right and what he demands: 'See that justice is done, let mercy be your first concern, and humbly obey your God.'
MICAH 6:8

Bible links

- Isaiah 58 (a radical challenge to remove the chains of those who are oppressed, to share food with those who are hungry and to give clothes to those who need them)
- 1 John 3:18 (love with actions, not words)

Key focus: Campaigning and social action

Key group: Church family; families; local community; schools; uniformed groups

Activity ideas

Select one of the MDGs as a focus area of action. The choice may be determined by someone in the church family or local community having a particular interest or passion for one of the areas. Use the Micah Challenge website to research some of the current campaigns. Pray about the possible responses to this information.

If you are able to work with a local primary school, a suitable focus might be to promote universal primary education, for example. For this you could research ways of supporting a particular school or an area where many children do not have the opportunity to go to school. Organise a fund-raising event that highlights the needs of the place to be supported. For example, organise a lunch or supper that serves food from the country in question. Have a quiz about the country so that people can learn more. Get someone to talk about the need. Ask the primary school in your area to use the internet to research life in the country you are going to support and create a PowerPoint display. Charities such as Embrace the Middle East, World Vision and Compassion UK have funding programmes for educational projects. Giving money to one of these would help ensure that the donation is used where it is particularly needed.

While fund-raising is a key part of the Micah Challenge, we are also invited to become 'prayer warriors' to support their campaign. Ensure that intercessions relating to your chosen MDG are regularly included in main services and in events where children get the opportunity to pray. This will work best if someone acts as a 'prayer warrior champion' to maintain a regular flow of information to those who will be leading intercessions.

The third aspect of the Micah Challenge is to change our own habits. How, as a church family, school or uniformed group, can we ensure that the way we live does not involve the degradation of those who grow our food, sew our clothes or make our footballs? Some churches may choose to provide a series of Bible study materials for home groups to look at the issues—visit the Micah

Challenge website for background material. Others may highlight one small change each month that people can make to work for a fairer world. Children have a highly developed sense of justice, and many will feel called to take action.

— Prayer —

Lord God, you have told us what is right and we want to try to do what you ask of us. Inspire and strengthen us to see that justice is done. Let mercy be our first concern, and may we humbly obey you, our God.

(BASED ON MICAH 6:8)

Developing the theme

Keep going! After a month or two of focusing on one MDG, look to another. Find another appropriate charity to support. Remind people of the words of the prophet Micah: 'The Lord God has told us what is right and what he demands: "See that justice is done, let mercy be your first concern, and humbly obey your God."' And just do it!

* * *

Movie sing-along

Date: anytime

Web link

www.ccli.co.uk/licences/churches_showing-entire-films.cfm

Introduction

There are some movies that are great to sing along with. *The Sound of Music* has great, memorable songs and sound theology. Invite everyone to come along in fancy dress and offer Austrian-style refreshments such as hot chocolate topped with whipped cream and Apfel Strudel.

Other possible titles are *Joseph and the Amazing Technicolor Dreamcoat* (to share a Bible story and another chance to dress up); as well as *Oliver*, *Mary Poppins*, *High School Musical* and *Jungle Book*. If the movie does not suggest specific refreshments, popcorn and fizzy drinks are always popular. *Mamma Mia* is also popular, although the subject content and some of the language used might make this film less suitable for family viewing with younger children. For *Mamma Mia* someone must be primed (and rehearsed) with a whistle to blast out the one specific swear word in the film.

It is essential that the church has both a Church Video Licence and a Performing Rights Society for Music Church Licence to show movies. Be aware that the Christian Copyright Licensing scheme does not permit you to charge to show films. If you need to charge for anything, make it clear that people are paying for refreshments (although it is far better not to charge at all). This kind of event could also be used to raise money for charity.

Key Bible verse

Sing a new song. Shout! Play beautiful music.
PSALM 33:3

Bible link

• Jeremiah 31:13 (all ages will celebrate together)

Key focus: Fun; fund-raising for charity

Key group: Church family; local community; families

Activity ideas

Once you have decided what movie to show, arrange for a few people to dress up in appropriate costumes. Take a photograph and use this in your publicity. Contact the local paper and radio to publicise the event, and make sure that local primary schools are given details too. Emphasise that everyone will be encouraged to participate as fully as possible. It may be possible to offer prizes for the best fancy dress. You may wish to offer a 'learn the songs in advance' workshop. This could take place after school or the previous weekend to the event. Use a CD to provide the music if you do not have a pianist available.

If you have the resources, show a few brief 'adverts' at the beginning of the event to help reproduce the cinema experience. These 'adverts' could be for church services as well as for other events you have planned. Next, organise a fancy dress parade. If you are showing *The Sound of Music*, invite people to parade in different categories (Maria, children, Captain von Trapp, nuns and so on) and finish with the quirky interpretations that some people will have created such as 'a ray of golden sun' or 'raindrops on roses'. Invite someone impartial to pick a few winners and hand out some small prizes. Then stop for refreshments if the movie does not have an intermission. *The Sound of Music* is long, so it is better to have the refreshment break halfway through so that legs can be stretched.

Avoid providing a homily or sermon at the end of the performance. People have come along to watch a movie. They will not return for the next screening if they feel they have been preached at.

— Prayer —

Creator God, thank you for the creativity of movie makers. Help us to build community as we share the fun of enjoying a film together.

Developing the theme

If the first sing-along goes well, this could become a termly event. It is possible to repeat a popular movie after a year. For example, before reshowing *The Sound of Music*, offer an activity session where people can make Apfel Strudel, create a banner to illustrate key scenes in the film, make spoon puppets to wave during 'The Lonely Goatherd', and offer face-painting with the design of 'whiskers on kittens'. Invite everyone to list or draw their favourite thing. There may be someone who can teach people to dance the Ländler or lead them in an energetic parade around the room to 'Doh, a deer', to provide a physical activity!

* * *

Preschool or nursery project

Date: anytime

Web link

www.ci2eye.co.uk (the website for Ci2Eye, Christian Initiatives in Early Years Education, an organisation which can provide valuable advice in this area)

Introduction

The encouragement of pretend play is a major part of educational provision for young children. This idea encourages a preschool to bring children to visit the church building and the church, then provides materials to stimulate imaginative play. Rather than telling the preschool what to do, the aim is to provide everything that will be needed. I am grateful to Ellie Wilson, Under 5s Adviser for the Diocese of Wakefield, for some of the ideas.

Key Bible verse

Let's walk around Zion and count its towers. We will see its strong walls and visit each fortress. Then you can say to future generations, 'Our God is like this forever and will always guide us.'

PSALM 48:12–14

Bible link

• Psalm 78:4 (tell the next generation)

Key focus: Sharing the Christian story; providing sacred space for reflection

Key group: Nurseries; preschools and schools

Activity ideas

Offer to create a 'church' imaginative play area for a short season in a preschool or nursery. Most nurseries provide a changing imaginative play area through the year. Themes can include a doctor's surgery or hospital, a vet's surgery, a travel agent, a shop, a beach or other places that children have visited. Explain that you would like to invite the children to visit the church to look around and then provide play facilities for them to role-play their visit. At this stage check the amount of space available and any restrictions as to what might be provided. Discuss with the leaders if it is possible to link the church visit and play space with any topic they have planned. For example, if they will be looking at 'My family' or 'Beginnings', then it would be good to focus the visit on baptism or weddings. Equally, 'My family' or 'Food' would suggest a focus on Holy Communion.

Use large cartons to build some walls. These could be painted grey or a colour to match the local church. Then use black to create the outline of bricks or stone blocks. Ensure that the walls are secure when assembled. For the inside of the 'church', provide a low table to represent the altar and a cloth to cover it—the aim is to make it as similar to what the children saw on their visit as possible. If the children met a robed priest, provide some simple robes for them to dress up. At the very least, provide a pretend stole or a preaching gown. If the minister showed the children the vessels used for Holy Communion, provide safe versions for the children to use in role play. For example, a plain wooden eggcup on a stem makes a good play-proof and unbreakable chalice and a simple small wooden plate will serve as a paten. Alternatively, if the visit included an imaginary baptism, provide a font, a suitably dressed baby doll and a shell scoop. Check whether the preschool is happy for the font to be filled with water as that may dictate the container used. For example, a large plastic mixing bowl could form the basis of a font that will contain water. Ensure that all the materials provided are suitable for small hands to manipulate. If the children saw service cards in use, provide a set for them to handle, and if they saw the baptism register, offer a similar book for them to write in.

Make sure that you provide enough materials and options for the children to explore in play what they have experienced. Preschools usually limit the number of children role-playing to fewer than six at a time, so it is not necessary to provide lots of sets of the same resources. However, you may need to provide extra supplies so that the resources can be replenished. Arrange to call in from time to time to tidy up the play church and make sure that all the kit looks clean and fresh.

— Prayer —

Father of all, help us to share your love with these precious children.
Guide us as we follow the instruction of your word to tell the next
generation about you.

Developing the theme

Offer a similar project to special schools that look after children with disabilities or learning difficulties. Again, try to tailor what you are able to offer to the planned curriculum of the school. This may mean that you have to wait for a year until an appropriate theme is being followed.

* * *

Random acts of kindness

Date: anytime

Web links

www.randomactsofkindness.org
http://en.wikipedia.org/wiki/Random_act_of_kindness

Introduction

For Jewish people, one of the meanings of mitzvah includes a good deed or an act of kindness. The earliest mention of random acts of kindness seems to date from the early 1980s. Now the concept is so well developed that random acts of kindness have been included in films, such as *Evan Almighty*, radio and television shows.

Key Bible verse

Treat everyone with kindness.
1 PETER 3:9

Bible links

- Genesis 24:1–26 (Rebecca draws water for Abraham's servant)
- Job 10:12 (God showers us with kindness)
- John 12:3 (Mary of Bethany anoints Jesus with perfume)
- Ephesians 3:16 (God treats us with kindness)
- Philemon 14 (acts of kindness should come from the heart)

Key focus: Campaigning and social action; fun

Key group: Church family; families; local community; schools; uniformed groups

Activity ideas

Set a date for a focus week for everyone to perform their random acts of kindness. This could be launched at a church service, at which everyone is commissioned and prayed for, or by a special assembly in school. A suitable Bible passage to use to highlight the 'randomness' of the idea might be the story of Mary's anointing Jesus' feet with perfume. An Old Testament story might be Rebecca's offering to bring water for the camels of Abraham's servant even though he had asked for water only for himself.

Give some examples of actions such as the following ideas.

Ideas of actions for individuals

- Holding open a door for someone pushing a wheelchair or buggy
- Allowing someone to go ahead of you in a queue
- Making hot drinks for everyone in your workplace
- Smiling at ten people you don't know
- Taking flowers or a pot plant to work, your favourite coffee shop or someone who is housebound
- Sweeping the path for someone who cannot manage it themselves
- Returning an abandoned shopping trolley to its home

Ideas of actions for groups

- Clear litter in a small area (protective gloves, sacks and litter pickers can be borrowed from the local council)
- Tidy the garden of an elderly person or a single-parent family
- Redecorate a room for a community preschool
- Distribute small bars of Fairtrade chocolate outside a railway or bus station
- Visit a residential home to provide musical entertainment for residents

Invite everyone to record, anonymously, the kind acts they have done on a large graffiti sheet or by writing on to paper leaves to be tied to bare branches to bring them to life. Recording the acts of kindness will encourage everyone by the sheer number of actions being carried out. At the end of the week, give thanks for all the acts of kindness and the people who have done them, and pray for all the people who have received them.

— Prayer —

Lord of all life, you have showered us with kindness and watched over us. Inspire us to shower kindness on those whom you bring to our notice. Give us the courage to be extravagantly kind.

(BASED ON JOB 10:12)

Developing the theme

This could start as an Advent or Lent project in the first instance but then be repeated once a quarter. Keep everyone's interest by having a designated week for the activity rather than expecting people just to keep going. However, it is likely that people who take part will find that they are performing more and more random acts throughout the year as it becomes established as a good way to behave.

* * *

TwoToo

Date: anytime

Web link

www.twotoo.co.uk

Introduction

Many of us love to shop and this idea gives us the opportunity to shop for two!

Key Bible verse

You are better off to have a friend than to be all alone, because then you will get more enjoyment out of what you earn. If you fall, your friend can help you up. But if you fall without having a friend nearby, you are really in trouble. … As the saying goes, 'A rope made from three strands of cord is hard to break.'

ECCLESIASTES 4:9–10, 12

Bible link

• Ecclesiastes 11:1–2 (Be generous and share what you have)

Key focus: Building community relationships; fun; campaigning and social action

Key group: Church family; families; local community

Activity ideas

Spend money on yourself, and encourage your church or groups in your local community to spend money on themselves—but to do it in a way that benefits other people at the same time. Visit the TwoToo website to find out how people can buy a gorgeous scarf or hoodie for themselves or as a present for a friend. TwoToo then give a scarf, funded by your purchase, to a homeless person. As they say on their website: 'TwoToo is the opposite of most designer labels. Instead of implying exclusivity and superiority it expresses support and identification with those in need... a little touch of equality in an unequal world.' After all, why buy just one scarf when you can buy two!

Publicise the TwoToo project in the church. Then ask anyone who uses social media to tweet about the website or to include a link on their Facebook page.

Prayer

Look at the scarf and thank God for the hands that made it. Drape the scarf round your neck, feel its warmth and imagine the person out on the street wearing the scarf for which you have paid. Pray for that unknown person; for safety, for food, for companionship, for hope. Continue to pray for them whenever you use your scarf.

Developing the theme

If there is a Soup Run or similar project for homeless people in your area, TwoToo are also interested in hearing from you, so that they can distribute scarves in different areas.

Appendices

*

Generic games

Duck, duck, goose

Players sit in a circle facing inwards. The person chosen to be 'It' walks around the outside of the circle gently tapping each player's head in turn saying 'duck'. When he or she says 'goose' instead of 'duck', that player has to stand up and race round the circle to try to tag the person playing 'It' before he or she has raced ahead to sit in the empty place. Different objects to illustrate an event's theme can be used as the command words.

Hot potato

Players stand in a circle and pass a potato round as the music plays. When the music stops, whoever is holding the 'hot' potato has to drop out.

Hunt the thimble

Hide a small object beforehand. Invite everyone to search. After a few minutes, if anyone gets close to the hiding place say 'Warm' and as they get closer say 'Warmer' or even 'Hot'. If they move away from the object say 'Getting colder'. This helps the searchers move towards where they should be looking.

Kim's game

Place up to 20 items on to a tray and cover over with a cloth. When everyone is ready, remove the cloth and encourage everyone to memorise the items they can see. After two minutes, re-cover the tray and take it away. While no one can see, remove two items from the tray. Bring the covered tray back into the group and challenge them to identify which items are now missing. Alternatively, during the two minutes, challenge everyone to work individually or in small teams to write down as many items as they can remember from the tray. The individual or team with the highest number of correctly remembered items wins the game.

Megaphone

Divide the group into two teams, A and B. Half of Group A stand in a line down one side of the room, and the other half stand facing them on the other side of the room. Group B are split up in the same way, but have to stand alternately in between Group A players. Then give the leader of the first half of Group A a short, simple Bible verse and a similar but different Bible verse to the leader of the first half of Group B. The players with the Bible verses share it with their half of their group. On the signal to start, the half of the groups that has been given a Bible verse have to shout it out so that the rest of their group on the other side of the room can try to work out what it is. The difficulty comes from Groups A and B having different verses to share while they are all shouting at the same time.

Pin the tail on the donkey

Provide a large picture of a donkey and fix it to a wall. One person at a time is given a paper tail with a blob of sticky tack to attach in the correct place on the donkey picture after they have been blindfolded. Turn older children and adults around at least twice after they have been blindfolded so they lose their awareness of where the picture is.

Port and starboard

Each corner of the room represents one item, place or person in the theme you are illustrating, and the centre of the room represents a fifth. When the leader calls out the name of an item, everyone has to run to that space. This game can be played competitively so that the last person to arrive at the corner is 'out'. Alternatively, it can be played as a way to learn the key people, places or elements of a Bible story with everyone moving around to the different spaces several times. For the Pumpkin Party, use relevant words such as 'seeds', 'flesh', 'sugar' and 'pastry', with 'pumpkin pie' as the key word for everyone to run into the centre.

Simon says

The leader calls out actions that everyone has to perform. Any moves should be made only if the leader first says 'Simon says' or another phrase of command. The most obvious command phrase could be 'Jesus says'. If the command phrase is omitted, no one should make a move, otherwise they are 'out'.

Sleeping lions

Everyone lies on the floor and pretends to be asleep. Anyone who can be seen to move or heard to make any noise is eliminated. This is a good game to help everyone to calm down. It can be used to illustrate the three young women being asleep when St Nicholas provides money for their dowry.

Telephone (also known as Chinese Whispers)

The leader gives a secret message to one person. They then have to whisper the message to the next person in the line and so on. The last person returns to the leader to give them the message back. This can be played competitively with two or more circles of people passing on the message. The winning group is the one that redelivers the message as close to the original form as possible.

What's the time, Mr Wolf?

One player is Mr Wolf and stands at the end of the room facing the wall. The rest of the players stand at the other end of the room. Someone calls out, 'What's the time, Mr Wolf?' and Mr Wolf answers with a time. If Mr Wolf says '2 o'clock' then the players can take two steps forward or if Mr Wolf says '10 o'clock', they can take ten steps forward and so on. The aim is for one of the players to get up to Mr Wolf and touch him or her without being caught. But at any point Mr Wolf can answer 'Dinner time' and turn round to chase the players to try to catch one of them before they get back to the safety of their starting place.

Suggested songs

Be still, for the presence of the Lord (*Hymns Old and New* 60)

Come all you people, come and praise your maker (*Songs of Fellowship* 1201)

Easter Jubilation (*Songs for Every Easter* 5)

Father, hear the prayer we offer (*Hymns Old and New* 141)

For God so loved the world (John Hardwick)

He's got the whole world in his hands (*Hymns Old and New* 268)

Jesus' love is very wonderful (*Kidsource* 208)

Lord of the dance (*Hymns Old and New* 290)

Loving shepherd of thy sheep (*Hymns Old and New* 432)

My God is so big, so strong and so mighty (*Kidsource* 255)

One more step along the world I go (*Hymns Old and New* 510)

Our Father, who art in heaven (Caribbean Lord's Prayer) (*Come and Praise* 51)

Our God is a great big God (*Junior Praise* 589)

Shout for joy and sing (*The Source* 450)

Such love (*Hymns Old and New* 600)

The king of love my shepherd is (*Hymns Old and New* 634)

The Lord's my shepherd (*Hymns Old and New* 636)

The Lord's my shepherd (I will trust in him alone) (*Hymns Old and New* 637)

The Virgin Mary had a baby boy (*Hymns Old and New* 654)

We have a king who rides a donkey (*Junior Praise* 264)

When I think about the cross (*Songs for Every Easter* 10)

Will you come and follow me (*Hymns Old and New* 740)

✳

Suppliers

Good Shepherd Sunday (see page 29)

Find pipe cleaners, the slightly larger chenille sticks, and self-adhesive eyes at: www.ss-services.co.uk

Crazy Bible hats (see page 171)

Find cheap plastic bowler hats, which could form the base for these, at a party supplier such as: www.partytracker.co.uk

Board game: The life and work of Paul

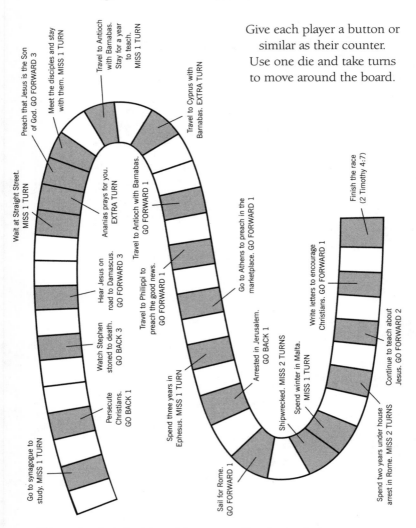

Give each player a button or similar as their counter. Use one die and take turns to move around the board.

Travel to Antioch with Barnabas. Stay for a year to teach. MISS 1 TURN

Meet the disciples and stay with them. MISS 1 TURN

Preach that Jesus is the Son of God. GO FORWARD 3

Travel to Cyprus with Barnabas. EXTRA TURN

Wait at Straight Street. MISS 1 TURN

Ananias prays for you. EXTRA TURN

Travel to Antioch with Barnabas. GO FORWARD 1

Hear Jesus on road to Damascus. GO FORWARD 3

Travel to Philippi to preach the good news. GO FORWARD 1

Go to Athens to preach in the marketplace. GO FORWARD 1

Finish the race (2 Timothy 4:7)

Watch Stephen stoned to death. GO BACK 3

Write letters to encourage Christians. GO FORWARD 1

Arrested in Jerusalem. GO BACK 1

Persecute Christians. GO BACK 1

Spend three years in Ephesus. MISS 1 TURN

Shipwrecked. MISS 2 TURNS

Spend winter in Malta. MISS 1 TURN

Continue to teach about Jesus. GO FORWARD 2

Go to synagogue to study. MISS 1 TURN

Sail for Rome. GO FORWARD 1

Spend two years under house arrest in Rome. MISS 2 TURNS

Visit www.barnabasinchurches.org.uk/extra-resources/ for a free download.

196

*

Bibliography

Children's Bibles

The Action Bible, God's redemptive story, Sergio Cariello (David C. Cook, 2010)

The Barnabas Children's Bible, Rhona Davies (Barnabas for Children, 2012)

Great Bible Stories for Children Age 5 and Up, Jose Perez Montero (Scandinavia, 2009)

Further reading

All-Age Worship, Lucy Moore (BRF, 2010)

Post-modern Children's Ministry, Ivy Beckwith (Zondervan, 2004)

Spiritual Garments, Julie McGann (Decani Books, 2006)

Top Tips on Reaching Unchurched Children, Helen Franklin (Scripture Union, 2005)

Who Let The Dads Out?, Mark Chester (Barnabas for Children, 2012)

*

Index

Ideas

Key focus

Key groups

Key Bible verses

Prayer activities

Prayers involving making things

Prayers with movement or physical activity

Singing prayers

Prayers using objects

Creative Mission

Over 50 ideas for special days, celebrations, festivals, community-based projects and seasonal activities

Creative Mission sets out to demonstrate that mission is fun, practical, easy-to-do and, above all, possible. The book contains a wealth of ideas to help churches, large and small, urban and rural, to connect with people who have occasional contact with the church, as well as suggestions for the church family to join in community events.

Many of the ideas are for families, children and adults, to enjoy together or alongside one another. Some ideas can be used within worship; others are for social events, fundraising activities, campaigns for justice across the world or RE and assemblies in schools. All will appeal to children as well as adults, but many can also be used if there are few or no children in the church family.

The ideas are arranged in four sections to fit with the seasons of the year. Some follow the church calendar; others link with secular high points in the year such as Valentine's Day, Red Nose Day, Father's Day and 'Back to School'.

The suggestions are offered for both traditional churches and Fresh Expressions of church to select those that will work best for them and the community they serve.

ISBN 978 1 84101 806 5   £8.99
Available from your local Christian bookshop or direct from BRF:
www.barnabasinchurches.org.uk.

The Story of REinspired

Developing creative partnerships between churches
and schools

David Skinner, Paul Haynes and Jane Earl

REinspired tells the story of how a group of churches in Earley and East Reading developed a way of working with primary schools to support the teaching of RE. The material covers the background of how the project developed and explores the principles REinspired has worked to—including stories of how students have engaged with the materials, and how churches from a wide ecumenical base have been involved. It then provides a practical guide to enable others to use the model to develop links between their own church and local schools.

The REinspired story covers the development of RE and assembly materials; the recruitment and support of volunteers; how to build relationships with schools and others; and all the practical considerations the team have learnt so far on their journey.

The book aims to inspire and enable churches to become fully engaged in resourcing RE in schools. The structure provides plenty of help in terms of training and materials, and useful contacts and information about ongoing support.

ISBN 978 1 84101 771 6   £8.99
Available from your local Christian bookshop or direct from BRF:
www.barnabasinchurches.org.uk.

Creative Ideas for All-Age Church

12 through-the-year programmes for informal church services and special one-off events

Karen Bulley

The twelve themes in this book contain a wealth of creative worship ideas, all designed to encourage the church family to listen to each other's stories. Through listening and worshipping together in a less formal setting, the material promotes creative thinking and enables people of all ages to learn together in worship and grow in faith as part of God's family.

The themes can be used to plan stand-alone worship programmes or to follow the pattern of the Christian Year, giving an ideal opportunity for once-a-month exploration of colour, creativity and individuality of each season. Some themes are based on Bible stories or issues relevant to the church family, while others use abstract ideas designed to promote lateral thinking.

The material offers a wide range of practical ideas and fun (or reflective) activities designed to give choice to those planning the worship. A pick-and-mix approach provides flexibility for the length and setting of worship.

ISBN 978 1 84101 663 4   £7.99
Available from your local Christian bookshop or direct from BRF:
www.barnabasinchurches.org.uk.

The Big Story

36 session outlines and reflective stories exploring
six big themes of God's love

Martyn Payne

The Big Story contains a treasure bank of creative, visual storytelling sessions designed to unpack six big Bible themes. The approach connects up the whole story of the Bible and attempts to give an overview of God's purposes by seeing the Bible not as a collection of unrelated events but as an amazing and ordered revelation of God's love.

Each of the 36 sessions contains a wealth of thought-provoking activities and reflective ideas to accompany the storytelling. The material includes an initial overview in the form of a visual timeline of Bible history, designed to help children and their leaders gain the bigger perspective. The six themes are then each introduced by a reflective story that acts as an anchor for a further six individual stories. The material in *The Big Story* is ideal for 6- to 10-year-olds.

ISBN 978 1 84101 812 6   £10.99
Available from your local Christian bookshop or direct from BRF:
www.barnabasinchurches.org.uk.

Enjoyed

this book?

Write a review—we'd love to hear what you think.
Email: reviews@brf.org.uk

Keep up to date—receive details of our new books as they happen.
Sign up for email news and select your interest groups at:
www.brfonline.org.uk/findoutmore/

Follow us on Twitter @brfonline

By post—to receive new title information by post (UK only), complete
the form below and post to: BRF Mailing Lists, 15 The Chambers, Vineyard,
Abingdon, Oxfordshire, OX14 3FE

Your Details	
Name _____	
Address_____	
_____	
Town/City _____	Post Code _____
Email_____	

Your Interest Groups (*Please tick as appropriate)	
❏ Advent/Lent	❏ Messy Church
❏ Bible Reading & Study	❏ Pastoral
❏ Children's Books	❏ Prayer & Spirituality
❏ Discipleship	❏ Resources for Children's Church
❏ Leadership	❏ Resources for Schools

Support your local bookshop
Ask about their new title information schemes.